42 Rules for 24-Hour Success on LinkedIn

By Chris Muccio
with David Burns
and Peggy Murrah

E-mail: info@superstarpress.com
20660 Stevens Creek Blvd., Suite 210
Cupertino, CA 95014

First Printing: December 2008
Paperback ISBN: 978-1-60773-018-7 (1-60773-018-9)
Place of Publication: Silicon Valley, California, USA
Library of Congress Number: 2008940965

eBook ISBN: 978-1-60773-019-4 (1-60773-019-7)

Trademarks

All terms mentioned in this book that are known to be trademarks or service marks have been appropriately capitalized. Super Star Press™ cannot attest to the accuracy of this information. Use of a term in this book should not be regarded as affecting the validity of any trademark or service mark.

Warning and Disclaimer

Every effort has been made to make this book as complete and as accurate as possible, but no warranty of fitness is implied. The information provided is on an "as is" basis. The author, contributors, and publisher shall have neither liability nor responsibility to any person or entity with respect to any loss or damages arising from the information contained in the book. As of the time of this printing, none of the Authors has any formal business relationship with LinkedIn. LinkedIn has not endorsed this book.

If you do not wish to be bound by the above, you may return this book to the publisher for a full refund.

Praise For This Book!

"Reading this book will give you a solid foundation for your LinkedIn strategy!"
Jason Alba, CEO of JibberJobber.com and author of '*I'm on LinkedIn—Now What???*'

"Peggy, Chris, and David have created an easy-to-read and implement guide to LinkedIn that really does the job of getting you connected fast. In the social networking jungle, this is one of the best guides you'll find—for a site that reaches YOUR people!"
Suzanne Falter-Barns, http://getknownnow.com

"'42 Rules to 24 Hour Success on LinkedIn' provides straightforward, common sense advice on how to get the most out of LinkedIn—the most popular social networking site for busy professionals. In this compact book, Chris, David, and Peggy show you what to do to leverage the power of social networking on LinkedIn. And they do it in an easy to use, enjoyable read. If you want to build a network of likeminded professionals, you need to be on LinkedIn. If you're on LinkedIn you need to read 42 Rules to 24 Hour Success on LinkedIn."
Bud Bilanich, The Common Sense Guy, Bestselling author of '*Straight Talk for Success*'

"These 42 Rules provide entrepreneurs, corporations and job seekers with gems of advice and are the perfect resource to make sense of how you can generate success with LinkedIn. For new users, it provides a terrific overview and for experienced users, it is a great reminder of the things you may know intuitively but may have forgotten in the rush of our hectic schedules."
Michael Port, author of '*Book Yourself Solid & The Contrarian Effect*'

"The book is a very practical, yet easy and fun read. It is impressive in its clarity presenting the various aspects for generating 24-Hour success on LinkedIn without the typical hype. You will come away understanding the core business principles driving your LinkedIn success."
Mitch Meyerson, Founder of Guerrilla Marketing Coaching and author of '*Mastering Online Marketing*'
http://MitchMeyerson.com

"From a business perspective, social networking is changing every day with new technology, tools and strategies. With so many options at our fingertips, users are challenged simply trying to determine where to begin and how to effectively use these tools. Given this bewildering landscape, the book '42 Rules for 24-Hour Success on LinkedIn' ties it all together quite simply and provides excellent practical tips and advice as how to effectively embrace this change."
J. John Simione, Senior Vice President, MARSH,
http://marsh.com

"As an Executive providing counseling to hundreds of displaced employees annually, I am always looking for new ways to provide job seekers with leading edge tools to help make their searches more effective. This book nails it! It is a user-friendly roadmap for understanding the power of LinkedIn and helps move readers successfully along the path of their choosing. I highly recommend this to both clients and businesses!"
David Bennington, Vice President-Consulting Services, Right Management

"Amazing! In this timely and cutting-edge book, the authors share their secrets to increasing your ROI on your online networking efforts. They give an abundance of tips and strategies to develop relationships using LinkedIn. Learn how to automate and leverage relationships through Social Fusion. I strongly recommend this book to anyone that wants to increase their sales results. If you want to build visibility and develop profitable relationships, read this book!"
Rick S. Cooper, MBA, The Sales Results Expert,
http://rickscooper.com

"LinkedIn has quickly emerged as a powerful networking tool, and "42 Rules" is a terrific actionable guide to help the savvy professional leverage LinkedIn effectively. The Rules provide a strategic framework that enables the user to quickly build their LinkedIn network, and more importantly, use that network to drive their LinkedIn "brand" to deliver results, opportunities, and action."

Alex Sevilla, Assistant Dean & Director of MBA Programs; The University of Florida

Publisher

- Mitchell Levy
  http://superstarpress.com/

Executive Editor

- Laura Lowell
  http://42rules.com/

Cover Designer

- Cate Calson
  http://calsongraphics.com/

Layout

- Teclarity
  http://teclarity.com/

Contents

Contents

Intro

We all continue to hear the same phrases over and over again—I'm too overwhelmed, I'm too busy, I can't put my full attention to that, etc. To be honest, if you ask my family, I am right in there with the "time challenged" too. It seemed that increasing business success and finding more time went hand in hand... or so I thought. One day, when I met my buddy Pete at a coffee shop, he talked about a certain type of success and described it in rather simple terms. He described a little kid, sitting on a dock with his fishing rod in the water. The kid fishes for some time, but nothing happens. So at some point, he gets bored, decides to lay back and takes a nap while leaving his baited hook in the water. When he wakes up, he excitedly finds that he hooked a fish while he was sleeping. The reason why he was successful without having to be actively engaged was pretty straightforward. He prepared himself for success by doing the simple things—baiting the hook and putting the hook in the water.

I think that is a great metaphor for this book and social networking. This book is not about achieving success in 24 hours, rather it is about doing the simple things that set you up for the opportunity to achieve success 24 hours a day. social networking occurs globally, 24 hours a day, 7 days a week. I know that I have arisen on multiple occasions to find that people I used to work with from outside the USA had found my profile and were interested in reconnecting with me. Now that is what LinkedIn is about; a place to find people and a place to be found. It's all about leveraging a communication tool and it is up to you to determine how you will use this communication platform to create your success. This might range from the simple connecting with people you've lost contact with, to finding a new job, to finding new talented individuals to add to your business, to creating a new revenue channel.

Given the tough economic times and the hype of social media, social networking and of course, LinkedIn, there is a certain curiosity about this business potential that seems to be only lightly addressed. Since LinkedIn or any social network is a 24-Hour tool, to most effectively position yourself to achieve your success any time of the day or night, you need to be like the little kid who took a nap while fishing. You need to "bait your hook and put it in the water" and, to help you, we offer you our 42 rules. As there are a variety of users with a variety of ideas for their success, some of the rules we offer may apply to you while others may not. These are by no means the only rules, so feel free to share them, discuss them, refine them and create new ones. Most important-ly, please keep in mind the most basic rule-simple preparation, just like our little fisherman learned, enhances your chances for 24-Hour success!

Section I
Setting Up Your Foundation

GOAL: Create a clear understanding for why you are using LinkedIn, social networking and social media. Support it with a thoughtful strategy and a commitment of time.

1 Rules are Meant to be Broken

What makes us different, makes LinkedIn great!

Who is the typical LinkedIn user? If you go by demographics, then it is a 41-year-old who has a household income of $109,000. However that doesn't tell the whole story. LinkedIn claims a membership that is growing at a rate of 30 people per minute, yet there really is not a typical "user." If you look around, you will find people who work solo and use LinkedIn as the proverbial office water cooler—a place to go to interact, share stories and be part of a community. This type of user might be using LinkedIn for personal and social development.

Then there are the people who create their own income. This can range from the one-person independent consultant to the managing partner of a consulting practice, from the small business owner to the commissioned sales professional. It includes everyone who generates his or her own income streams. Yes, they encounter a significant amount of risk, but they also tend to lean to an entrepreneurial way of thinking as they prospect for new, efficient and effective ways to generate revenue streams. Their interest generally lies in business development.

Shifting the risk profile, you also shift the perspective of the user to those who prefer the stability of a steady income. This can include anyone from the job seeker to the professional looking to manage a career path. While these people may have entrepreneurial inclinations, their income stream is not dependent on generating new sales. Instead it is dependent on their ability to manage, lead, work in groups, build relationships and generally help their employer in an effective manner. Any dollar they add to the business, they generally don't see. While they may understand that communication on LinkedIn can drive additional revenue, it is not their priority for participating on LinkedIn. Their priority is to stay plugged into a professional network that can help them leverage their career development.

What makes us different, makes LinkedIn great! The one commonality is that all these users are looking for some sort of development and benefit from LinkedIn yet, clearly, benefiting from LinkedIn means something different to almost every person.

As you read through this book, our rules take an approach that does not try to be everything to everyone. Instead, we follow a natural strategic development process where concepts build upon themselves. Not all the rules are going to apply to each type of user and, even for those that do, there may be a variety of ways to achieve similar results. So while we don't advocate going against the netiquette and norms established throughout social media, we do expect that you will use the rules as a flexible guide and bend or even break them if you see more effective ways to achieve a particular goal.

To further increase the effectiveness of this book for you, we have created a free downloadable workbook that you can find at http://LinkToProsper.com/24hoursuccess. This workbook is a stand-alone resource as well as a companion for these 42 rules. You will find a wide range of tips, questions, comments, etc. that will help you support your 24-Hour success!

2 Answer the Most Important Questions First

LinkedIn is a communication tool. It is a place to find people and be found.

Let's start with a question, *Why are you on LinkedIn?*

On the surface, this seems to be a simple question: only five words and none were more than 10 letters long. But it seems that whenever we ask that question, we're asking something on par with an existential question like, "What is the meaning of life?" because the response we get nine times out of ten is a contemplative silence. So we try to break the uneasy silence by asking another question, "What was your encouragement to register on LinkedIn?" and with that usually a big smile appears and they say, "Oh, I received an invitation to sign up." To which our reply is, "That's great, what are your goals for being registered on LinkedIn?" This time the responses range from that contemplative silence to the ambitious, "Gain more clients."

LinkedIn is a place for business professionals to be "found" and "to find" people. It is a vehicle to communicate. It is a tool to use with your business, in your career management, your education, your social endeavors and probably a whole lot more. Yes, you can turn contacts into clients and yes, you can turn prospects into customers but by itself, LinkedIn is not a magic elixir.

In simple terms, LinkedIn is a conduit; it is a connector. The people who receive the greatest results understand this and use LinkedIn accordingly. If you asked some of the people who have achieved successes with LinkedIn how they would define one formula for LinkedIn success, it would be similar to the following:

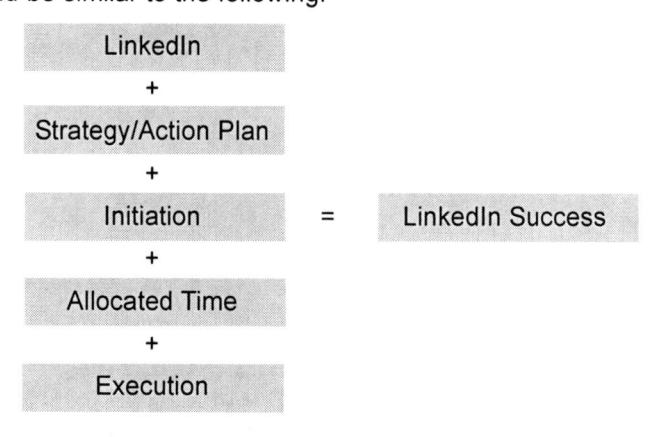

LinkedIn
+
Strategy/Action Plan
+
Initiation   =   LinkedIn Success
+
Allocated Time
+
Execution

So as we begin this book, we pose some questions for you to think about.

- Why are you on LinkedIn? Do you understand how you can most effectively benefit from it?

- What are you looking to achieve with LinkedIn? Are your goals realistic? Have you created a strategy and supported it with realistic action items?

- How are you showing initiative? You are reading these rules, so that indicates that you have the drive and commitment to learn. What else are you doing to enhance your ability to achieve the goals you've established on LinkedIn? For instance, if you are on it to network, are you networking? What have you been doing to build relationships?

- How much time are you fitting into your schedule to properly participate and execute on your strategy? Unfortunately, this is not the field of dreams (i.e. build it and they will come). Without allocating time in your busy schedule to work your action plan, you may end up more like a billboard in a jungle, bright and shiny but not seen by many people.

To reiterate, success on LinkedIn is not like rubbing the magic lantern and having the genie immediately appear. 24-Hour success should not imply immediate gratification. What 24-Hour success implies is literally setting yourself up for success by doing all the "right" things that will eventually help you succeed. In the wired world we live in, success can occur during the middle of the business day, when you are sitting in front of your computer or while you are sleeping in bed.

3 Get LinkedIn or Get Left Out?

Success is not based on what you know, but rather, who you know.

The old cliché is that success is not based on what you know, but rather, who you know. Understanding your online identity is critical to creating success, and LinkedIn is currently one of the more powerful tools that can help you. The challenge is how to learn the most effective ways to use LinkedIn without wasting time navigating the help functions, the online forums or Googling the gurus.

In typical day-to-day, face-to-face networking, when people are asked about their usage of LinkedIn, it seems that most people share the same experience. They sign up for LinkedIn, gather some contacts, and search out people they may know from schools, prior employers, or from professional associations. Once they've tapped that out, they are lost as to what to do next or how to realize any benefit from being on LinkedIn.

As successful professionals, your time is valuable and what you choose to focus on must provide you with an effective result. Therefore, as you begin reading this book, let's start off with some quick and immediate tips to help you dramatically improve your understanding of the LinkedIn experience and build your base of useful contacts.

Focus on Relationship Building

The cornerstone for your success starts with ensuring your understanding of what successful networking really means. It is not the sleazy concept of dropping off a business card and then racing to someone else to repeat the process over and over again. That type of person merely wants you to hear about them. They could care less about spending time to get to know you. Pretty shallow, right? Why would you do business with someone who doesn't care about you? If that is your idea of networking, don't even bother with LinkedIn.

Networking is about building relationships and getting to know the other person and how you might be able to contribute to their success. Successful networkers build their own credibility through their actions, which in turn builds a comfort level with the other party. This increased level of comfort leads to a stronger relationship. So, would you rather have business dealings with someone who is shallow or someone you've developed a relationship with? Relationship building should be the focus of your perspective and participation in LinkedIn.

Commit Time Weekly to Participate

This sounds like the most basic concept, but it is very important to adhere to it. Unfortunately many people join and collect contacts but invest no time or energy networking, so they gain nothing from the site. This is a clear example of reaping what you have sowed. Remember LinkedIn is just a tool to connect and open doors, but it still takes work on your part. Set aside at least an hour or so each week to invest in building your network.

Seek and Give Recommendations

One of the hardest things some people find is to adequately "brag" about their accomplishments. Whether you want to acknowledge it or not, you have probably compiled an impressive list of career successes. Having someone else "promote" your accomplishments is a very powerful tool. It builds your reputation and strengthens relationships as well as increases the value of your network to everyone connected to it.

LinkedIn offers Recommendations, which is a function that allows someone else to describe you and promote you to the world. Request recommendations from people who know you well and will best describe your strengths, achievements, etc. On the flip side, make sure you spread the recognition of people you know and recommend them. Remember, relationship building is a two-way street.

Consider the ROI

As these rules begin to increase your "knowledge portfolio," let's take a quick look at how you might consider *measuring Return on Investment* (ROI) for your online networking efforts. LinkedIn, of course, is the main *professional* social networking site but by no means the only one on the internet.

ROI is a common measurement that evaluates the amount of "benefit" derived from an investment. For instance, assume your social networking investment consists of spending five hours/week on LinkedIn. Now, let's assume your time is worth $200/hour. Across a year, your investment is roughly $50,000! *So... is it worth your time?*

Well... this is where it gets gray. The problem is that when it comes to measuring the ROI, returns are not direct and immediate. Thus the big question is... how do you properly measure a return from your activities?

Let's try to attack it from a financial analyst's standpoint. They are interested in annualized results (i.e. results that occur across a 12-month period). For example, assume in an average week, you connect with ten *new* people in addition to following up with 20 *existing* contacts. Thus, by the end of the year, you can directly attribute say, $30,000 of sales to your networking. Mathematically, for all your effort, your return looks like this (($30,000–$50,000)/$50,000) = -40%. Clearly a *negative return of 40%* is an outright failure, right? As Lee Corso (from ESPN's College Gameday) likes to say, "Not so fast, my friend." Why? Let's take a closer look.

First, while you have directly connected and followed up with people, you have undoubtedly also connected with an untold amount of people indirectly (friends of your connections, people who saw your communications, but didn't communicate directly with you, etc.). There is no way to calculate what benefits these returned. At the very least, one non-tangible benefit is establishing brand awareness for yourself. A more tangible but un-measurable benefit is that these "passive connections" more than likely contributed to your sales as well. Either way, this benefit is missing & can't be calculated but... it is still a benefit.

Second, the time it takes to build customer relationships varies. For some the time is immediate, while others need to work through their "marketing funnel," which may take a year or longer. Thus all those "long-termers" who take more than 12 months to show results (based on the calculation parameters above) are not captured either... but they too provide benefits.

The point is clear, or in this case, sort of a foggy gray, that measuring your ROI from social networking is difficult. So, short of giving away a free car to everyone to encourage a direct response, is there anything one can look at to determine if they are getting the "Bang for their social networking buck?"

Perhaps the most effective way to measure an ROI most tangibly is to measure the following:

- Web Traffic – Measure it & look for web traffic growth.
- New Links – Focus on the number of new links your website/blog, etc. receives. Depending on the quality of these links, you should see your search engine ranking improve modestly.
- Growth in your Opt-in Lists – Two things here – look at "total" growth as well as observe the growth trend from month to month. Expect increasing amounts of opt-ins, the longer you continue using effective tactics.
- Credibility Components – Expect an increase in the number of "authoritative elements" in your "profile"—on LinkedIn, this could include: recommendations, questions answered, best answer, etc.

Occam's Razor states "all other things being equal, the simplest solution is the best." However in this case, that doesn't fit. The simplest solution to measuring the ROI in social networking may be misleading. The astute social networker will include the above elements to provide the most effective measurement from the benefits of your social networking endeavors.

Rule

5 Optimize Your Activities

Social media will change your business; catch up or catch you later.

Business Week had a great headline with a recent article, "Social Media Will Change Your Business, Catch Up or Catch you Later." It's a great headline in that it is both catchy and true! We know some of the more famous elements of social media—LinkedIn, Facebook, YouTube, Digg, Technorati, and of course, there are literally hundreds more.

Let's narrow our focus for this rule to LinkedIn. In Rule 4, we looked at Return on Investment from your social networking activities, and here we look at optimizing your activities. With millions of users and growing daily, LinkedIn offers a variety of opportunities to quickly connect with a vast audience to enhance the potential for your career and business success. So how does one go about being "optimized?"

Simply put, social media optimization is doing what you need to be doing everyday with your interactions within your social marketing spheres. Simple concept...but it demands a lot of time and a lot of effort. To help, we will highlight four things you need to know to optimize and grow!

People base their buying decisions on experiences other people have had

Social marketing sites have become the new mainstream media of the marketing age. Your presence allows you to interact with your customers and help enhance their experiences with you. Keep in mind that more and more searches are being refined to be searches based on experiences. Since your customers are going to talk about their experiences, make sure you provide them with something positive to talk about.

Social media offers effective low-cost ways to market your business

Social media helps you start the conversation with people who may be looking at you. You can get your message out to millions of people at a time at a very low cost or even for free. For instance, you can post a video on YouTube and provide a link to it on LinkedIn or link your blog to your LinkedIn profile or answer consumer questions through LinkedIn Answers or... the list is limited only by your creativity.

Grow your audience using the "CAP" Approach

With millions of users on LinkedIn, how can you begin to transition from being a "billboard in a jungle" to being "a LinkedIn magnet?" One way would be to follow the CAP approach.

C = Content – People want new, they want unique, they want original, but what they don't want is boring. However LinkedIn provides a fairly boring standardized format, so it is up to you to use it creatively. Here are a couple of ideas: describe yourself in a manner that is clear, descriptive and interesting, use video links in your profile, and participate in group forums. Be as original as you can be.

A = Awareness – Make yourself known to search engines, RSS aggregators, listings, social networks, and fellow bloggers. Publish your URL appropriately when you post. The more times you articulate your message to more people, the more likely you are to find people who are interested in what you have to say.

P = Participate with Passion – Participate properly. If you don't, you can expect to become exactly like the "movie of the week," hot for a short time and then totally forgotten.

Leverage External Resources

Optimization can be very time consuming. The most common tasks are the most time consuming. Look for ways to outsource this.

If you need a recommendation for a Virtual Assistant (VA), try http://peggymurrah.com/. They've offered VA services since 1999, which is ancient in internet years, and have been providing quality services ever since.

6 Overcome the Overwhelm

Many people are struggling to understand where to begin and just as many are simply trying to find out how to properly participate.

By now, based on the hype, we are all somewhat aware of the potential that Web 2.0/Social Networks can offer you. However, after speaking to various groups of people, two things are becoming very apparent; many people are struggling to understand where to begin and just as many are simply trying to find out how to properly participate. In this rule, we will offer you "quick-start" guidance to help minimize your feeling of being overwhelmed, and guide you through the "participation puzzle."

social networking opens up a whole new level of contact with your prospects, your customers, your business partners and your employees. The elegance of social networking is the way it enables constant yet non-intrusive communication regarding literally anything your business needs to communicate about. So the benefits are clear, yet many of us are struggling to come to terms with the following:

ISSUE - Not Sure How to Participate / Afraid of Being Blackballed – There are many nuances to participating on various social networking sites, and they too seem to change daily. Most of these sites are communities where people have invested long hours into participating. You may even say, they've invested part of their lives into these sites. Given these investments, they don't take it lightly if someone jumps in and doesn't properly participate.

QUICK START GUIDANCE – Netiquette is important here. We advocate taking some time to get the lay of the land. Read through the FAQs, check out the "power users" and use the search engine to read up on what others say about the site.

ISSUE - Trying to Figure Out How to Get Positive Attention – Getting attention is probably the most important thing you can do in this Web 2.0 world and also the most competitive. Not only are you competing for attention from the social media world, but you are competing with the offline world as well. We've already estimated that there are hundreds, if not thousands, of sites out there with thousands of users on each site. In addition to that, there are 225 billion pages of editorial content pumped out every year. Given this, how valuable is attention? Think of Paris Hilton. What exactly does she do? One thing is for certain and that is—she gets attention. According to Forbes, last year she made a cool $6.3 million, received 3,600,000 web hits and was mentioned in almost 18,000 press clippings. Clearly attention is valuable.

QUICK START GUIDANCE – We advocate following the *CAP* principle (see Rule 5)

ISSUE - You Don't Have the Time to Devote to This – It goes without saying that in today's fast-paced information age, everyone is multi-tasking and there is little time available for anything new. Need we say more on this topic? Can you identify with the phrase "I'm in over-whelm—have to get out of it fast?"

QUICK START GUIDANCE – So is this a deal breaker?

Actually *No*—you can make time if you step back and think about this logically. Remember your first step? You were being strategic as to which sites you participated in. Some sites are more time-intensive than others. However, if you laid out your goals for these sites and supported them with realistic action plans, then all you need to do is "measure" your execution and continually tweak it to be more effective. Thus what you might be looking at is spending 15 minutes a day on LinkedIn, or five minutes a day on Twitter or an hour a week launching videos on YouTube. The point is if you understand what you are focusing on building, you can maximize your results without sacrificing more time.

Section II
What LinkedIn Offers

GOAL: Generate a high level perspective of ways that LinkedIn can offer opportunities for success for Businesses, Job Seekers, and those seeking Candidates.

7 Success Starts With a Clear Understanding of Your Goal

The definition of "user success" will vary from user to user.

LinkedIn is a powerful tool because of its incredible opportunity to network with other people and professionals. As was noted in Rule 1, there is no "typical user" per se, instead there is a variety of users from all over the globe across a variety of industries who all plug into LinkedIn. As the diversity is broad across LinkedIn, so is the definition of "user success," which will vary from user to user.

Success through Gaining Knowledge

Many people receive benefits from LinkedIn Answers, which is a database of questions that users can read and respond to. It's a lot like tapping into one's own informal board of advisors. It's a free place to go to get answers to questions that previously may not have been addressed due to a lack of knowledgeable resources. It's also a place that can help stimulate ideas. A friend recently told us of excellent advice he received in response to a question he posed. He was interested in using viral marketing to increase revenues and was looking forward to applying the advice he received in his pursuit of business success.

Success through Enhancing Credibility

Conversely, by answering questions, users have opportunities to provide advice that highlights their expertise. Since it is easy to see the profiles of the person giving the answers, providing answers is also a great way to promote a user's profile. To be fair, it isn't the end all, be all. To achieve success, you need to consistently work on providing answers that enable you to showcase your talents, which in turn enables you to promote yourself.

Success is Finding a Job, a Candidate or Strengthening Career Management

At a recent lunch, an acquaintance shared his success in landing a new position and told us, "I had no idea the opportunity was available. I received a call out of the blue after a recruiter saw my profile which was identified by a mutual contact." For many, the most tangible use of LinkedIn is for their careers. Some people find jobs, others have jobs that find them; employers have a low-cost way of identifying talent and, of course, those interested in career management have a very effective tool in which to do so. It goes without saying how simple it is for recruiters to conduct more effective job searches across LinkedIn and for many, having an extra channel that passively enables them to learn about new career opportunities is exactly what they are looking for.

Success is Meeting and Reconnecting with People

LinkedIn is a social network. Thus by definition, users should expect to interact socially. For many LinkedIn users, this is all they want to do. Prior to the advent of the online social networks, keeping in touch with people from one's past was very time-consuming. In many cases, it was difficult or impossible to reconnect. Thus, losing contact with former colleagues, friends and classmates was something that was an unfortunate byproduct of a person's growth. However, social networks have begun to eliminate the difficulty in reconnecting with these people and, as millions are finding out, it is very exciting to reconnect and catch up with people from your past.

8 Communicate Constantly Without Being Annoying

LinkedIn isn't just your ordinary communication tool. Its elegance is in its passive communication capability.

If you were to stop and try to visualize what effective communication means, you might envision two people completely engaged in a conversation. Since it isn't always possible to meet and communicate with people face to face, certain business tools are used as communication surrogates. These include cell phones, faxes, emails, texts and now—LinkedIn.

As you move across the communication spectrum, you see that the need for two active participants to create effective communication decreases tremendously. For instance, for a phone call to be most effective, you need two people talking. However, this is a time consuming task. Often one party is not available or simply doesn't want to address a particular issue at that moment, so they don't take the call. Conversely, LinkedIn isn't just your ordinary communication tool. Its elegance is in its passive communication capability. Yes, there are still two participants, but the "writer" doesn't have to actively engage anyone to effectively communicate with any and all interested readers. So, how can constant communication help?

More professionals will be aware of your identity and the business that you have. LinkedIn is more than just another social networking site. It has millions of members worldwide and they are all professionals! When you add connections with people in the same business niche as you, you are providing those professionals with information about yourself and what you have to offer. By completely filling out your profile, interested readers get a bird's eye view of who you are and what you can do.

LinkedIn helps you get in touch with professionals who might need your services. When people start knowing you and your services and they start talking about you and your products, then you will see the power of word-of-mouth marketing on the internet. As long as you remain professional in your conduct and relationship with people, they begin to effectively promote your services.

One of the beautiful things about LinkedIn is the ability to note "what you are working on." If you take a look at various profiles, most people just ignore this function. Through our limited research (of simply asking people why they do), it would appear they avoid it because they:

- don't understand the value of it
- don't know how to properly use it
- don't really feel they have anything important to add
- really don't spend any time adjusting their profile at all

Let's spend another 30 seconds and get a better understanding of how this function could benefit you. Whenever you update "what are you working on," that update is passively broadcast to everyone in your network. Thus it shows up on everyone's LinkedIn home page without having to send them an email, make a phone call or otherwise disturb them. Since you want this function to remain a credible one for you, don't abuse it. If you note every time you go to the store to get a gallon of milk, your brand will suffer. Therefore, update it for only for events of significance that add to your brand. For instance, let people know about a new blog you set up or a new business deal you've landed or one you are pursuing. Who knows, perhaps someone in your network can help you in pursuit of that deal.

9 It's Never Too Early to Build Relationships

Social media is about new ways of communication, and communication is the foundation for relationship building.

Harvey MacKay nailed it with the title of his book on networking, "Dig Your Well Before You are Thirsty." Given the uncertain economic times, do you know for sure if your job is going to be there in 6 or 12 months? Since social media is about new ways of communication, and communication is the foundation for relationship building, do you know where to begin to properly launch a relationship-building campaign that could lead to your next position?

Most job searches today begin with a search of the online job boards. Statistically speaking though, less than 10% of people searching for jobs that way actually land them. Job searchers need to be trying other avenues as well. Some of the traditional ones include: networking, looking through help wanted ads, working with professional outplacement firms, like DBM or Right Management, and working with headhunters—to name a few. Now it's time to add LinkedIn and social networking to that list!

Once you have identified companies that you want to target, LinkedIn can quickly help you determine if you have any warm contacts into those companies. Here is a suggested list of tactics to follow:

- Using the list of companies that you've generated, search them on LinkedIn (all 500 of the Fortune 500 are on LinkedIn) and see which individuals show up in your search results.

- Split these individuals into two categories by looking through their profiles. Category #1 would consist of a list of people that are currently working at a particular company and Category #2 would be comprised of people who previously worked there. Don't get too crazy in terms of the size of your lists. Keep them manageable and focused on key relationships, relative to your expertise.
- Sort these lists based on your Tier 1 or 2 contacts.
- Next, research the profiles of your "best contacts," looking for key phrases on the type of work they do and jot notes down about their specific job functions.
- Now, armed with a little "intel," assuming you have an effective LinkedIn network, try to contact those whom you consider the most relevant people to your search within those companies. The key point here is: the warmer the contact, the better.

If you don't have a large network on LinkedIn, here are some additional tips you could follow.

Let's assume that you have identified a list of people on LinkedIn who seemed to be relevant to the type of position you're looking for. Now look for ways to make contact with them in a non-intrusive manner.

- See if any of them are using the LinkedIn Answers function—either asking or answering questions. Either way, try to provide an answer to these questions. This may get their attention.
- If not, read through their profiles and take another route—see who has recommended them and determine if there was any way for you to connect with the person doing the recommending via LinkedIn Answers or otherwise. If so, that could provide you a solid entrée to your "cold contact."
- Finally, see if your cold contacts participate in any of the LinkedIn Groups. If they do, try to join those groups and try to establish contact that way.

If you would like to connect with us, please follow the links to our profiles
http://LinkedIn.com/in/ChrisMuccio
http://LinkedIn.com/in/PeggyMurrah
http://LinkedIn.com/in/DavidCBurns

Send us an invite noting that you've read the book and we'd be very happy to accept your invitation.

10 Focus on Career Development

LinkedIn is more than just another social networking site on the internet. It can actually help you in your career development. With millions of professionals out there whom you can connect with, you can make your career grow with the help of LinkedIn and other professionals.

Your LinkedIn profile may be considered as your online resume

As a professional, your educational background, your organizational and company affiliations and other important professional information may be displayed in your LinkedIn profile. This way, other professionals and employers can easily learn about you and what you have to offer.

Optimize your keywords

You can increase your visibility by adding keywords that are related to your profession and to what you do best as a professional. If employers, and people who are looking for a resource person related to your field, search by those keywords, you get a better chance of being the first person on the list.

Connect and grow your network

From your email address book, you can easily add friends to your LinkedIn network. You can also search friends who were employed by the same company you are connected with right now. There are a myriad strategies you will come across in some of the other rules. To maximize the effectiveness of your network, aim for at least 50 people in your first-degree connection.

Use LinkedIn Answers to the max.

Just like Yahoo Answers!, LinkedIn has LinkedIn Answers that allows people to post questions to the network. If you have any concern in your career development or in the way you do your work, you can just use this feature and solicit answers from all sorts of professionals in your network. You can also answer the questions posted by other people in the network so that people can notice what you know and what you have to offer.

Your action plan

Now it's your turn. Here are five things you can do to enhance your Job Search Process on LinkedIn.

- Job Search Jargon – use the search function to find people with similar skills to you and learn what jargon they used in their summary or in their professional description to be found on a search. Then incorporate that jargon into your profile.
- Interview Enhancement – learn about the people you will be interviewing with. For instance, let's say your research reveals you both went to the same college. Wouldn't information like this offer a great bonding opportunity?
- Reverse Reference Checks – prospective employers check on you. Now with LinkedIn, you can check on them and perhaps get the inside scoop from people who worked at a company.
- Stronger Employee Reference Checks – to supplement the glowing references prospective employees offer, you can find others who worked with them previously and get a balanced perspective.
- Company "Health" Assessment – do an assessment on the comings & goings of people at the company you are looking at. Check if there appears to be high turnover, strong prospects for career advancement, etc.

With its millions of users worldwide, LinkedIn is one of the best features of Web 2.0. It connects people and gives them a chance to get together for professional and work-related reasons.

11 Be Smart When Applying for Jobs

You have access to tons of information via LinkedIn that can help you position yourself and stand out from the crowd.

LinkedIn makes it easy to be really smart about the jobs you apply for. You have access to tons of information via LinkedIn that can help you position yourself and stand out from the crowd. To search for a job, go to the LinkedIn main menu located in the upper left corner of the screen. Click on the Jobs link. Next, enter keywords that describe the position, like Accountant or Project Manager or Human Resources Specialist. You can further refine your search by selecting Country or Zip code. Then click the blue Search link.

If you want to specify even more detail when conducting a job search, click the Advanced Search link located directly below the keywords box. On this page, you can specify the title, company, function and industry. You can also specify location, experience level, the time of posting and, optionally, enable a search by date of posting.

Once you click Search, you'll be supplied with a list of positions that meet your specified criteria. You'll see title, company, location, posting date and the name of the individual who created the posting. Select a job by clicking on the title. A page will open up that includes all the job detail. On the right side of the page, you'll see a box that says Posted By. At the bottom of the box, you'll see a link to Apply Now. Click the button and you'll be on your way.

Need a Job Referral

First, go to the page for a specific job you're interested in. On the right side, about half way down the page, you'll see a section called Inside Connections to the Company. Next, click on the name of the person who you want a referral from. Then go to the upper right corner of the screen and select Get Introduced through a Connection.

Alternatively, you can click on the job poster's name to apply directly to the job—if it's set up that way. Otherwise, you'll see a box located on the right, labelled Posted By. Below that you'll see the link Request Referral. Click on the link and you'll be on your way to finding someone in your own network through whom you can get a job referral.

Want an Inside Connection?

An Inside Connection is a connection to someone in your network of connections. When you're on the page for a particular job posting, you'll notice, on the right, a section that says Inside Connections to the Company. Click on one of the selections and you'll be taken to a list of people who are connected with that company or to people at that company in some fashion. You can use a LinkedIn Introduction to contact those individuals who may be two or three degrees from you.

To increase the chances you'll have an Inside Connection, invite more people to join your LinkedIn network. The more connections you have, the more likely they'll be connected to the individual who posted the job. More is better!

Confidentiality

Not to worry—no one has access to your resume except the job poster to whom you've actually emailed your resume.

12 It's More Than a Job Posting

When you post a job on LinkedIn, you get a lot richer perspective on the candidate. It's almost like "reality TV" for the hiring process.

When you're looking for a great candidate to add to your team, it's a good idea to tap into a variety of resources to find the best possible person. LinkedIn is a great resource for HR professionals and other recruiters who are looking to hire. When you post a job on LinkedIn, you get a lot richer perspective on the candidate. It's almost like "reality TV" for the hiring process as you can observe what candidates broadcast about themselves,—things like their profiles, their Answers, and their initiatives.

There is a fee for posting jobs. However, it is less expensive as compared with other online services. Since LinkedIn positions itself as a social networking site for business professionals, you might be able to find a better fit more quickly than you would by posting a similar position to a more generic job site.

It costs $195.00 to post a single job for 30 days. Every job you post will automatically expire after that time. You can renew your posting at any time for the same cost as the original posting, with each renewal providing you with an additional 30 days of online visibility.

You also have the option of purchasing "Job Credits" which allow you substantial savings if you buy a 5- or 10-package bundle of job posts. If you purchase five Job Credits, then each job posting costs you only $145.00. The 10 Job Credit package averages only $115.00 per posting—a substantial savings.

If you want to post a job, you just need to follow a few easy steps. First, go to the LinkedIn Menu located at the upper left on any LinkedIn page. Click on the "down arrow" located next to Jobs. Select Post a Job.

Fill out the job details. At the bottom of the online form, you can save a Draft so you can work on it later, or you can click on Next so you can review the details. Keep in mind that the job description is limited to 25,000 characters. Also, don't worry if you change any of the pre-populated inputs. This basic information is being pulled from your own LinkedIn profile. If you make any changes here on this information form, rest assured that your original profile will remain unchanged.

If everything is to your liking, click Post this Job to submit it to the system. You'll receive a confirmation that the job is posted and you're finished!

If you've posted a job on LinkedIn, anyone can view it. If the job is closed or if it expired, then you and any applicants will still be able to view it. If the job is deleted, it will not be viewable at all.

It's easy for others to apply to your job posting. They just need to click Apply to submit their resume. You'll receive the application at the email address you set up when you added the job posting. When you receive the information from the applicant, you'll be able to see their profile, all the information that they sent to you, as well as their relationship to you and your network.

Thanks to the wonders of technology, each time someone applies for a job you've posted, you'll automatically receive an email with their application. You can also check on your job applicants through the LinkedIn system. Go to the navigation bar in the upper left corner of any LinkedIn Page. Click on the drop-down arrow located next to Jobs. Select Manage Jobs and then you'll see the names of the applicants.

13 Precision is the Key to Business Development

There are many, many thousands of experienced professionals on LinkedIn whom you might not normally have access to, who will provide advice and career guidance.

LinkedIn is a business tool just like your cell phone or your PDA. However, it is not a magic elixir. It can function exceptionally well in a variety of ways but it can't be everything to everyone. Even with millions of users, people are still trying to figure out the most effective ways to use it. One thing is for sure; it functions best as a "precision-type" tool, (i.e. reach a specific person, learn a specific bit of info). If you are looking for something to "carpet bomb" and work as a mass market broadcast, there are more effective tools than LinkedIn.

LinkedIn can help connect professionals and business people via the internet. In addition, any individual or small business owner can tap into its "mentoring potential" and create their own "informal personal advisory board."

A tool like this should not be taken for granted and ignored. There are many, many thousands of experienced professionals on LinkedIn who will provide advice and career guidance that you might not normally have access to. Utilize LinkedIn Answers and ask the questions that can help you and your career prosper. They are really helpful, not only for the advice offered, but for the exposure to other people's thoughts and concepts that you might never have been exposed to otherwise. In many instances, tapping into this wealth of knowledge is invaluable.

The Yin to the Yang of the previous comment is to participate regularly on LinkedIn Answers and demonstrate your knowledge to the world. As we've stated previously, relationship building is a two-way street. Participating regularly in LinkedIn Answers is a great way to establish relationships, help or impress others and build up your contact lists. Make an effort to find and answer at least two questions per week.

social networking is about connecting others. One of the biggest questions that comes up is, "How can I use it for business development?" Here are a few ways that LinkedIn can help you with business development.

Prospect for Account Entry Points – Look for ways to generate warm introductions based on your network. For companies you are looking to prospect with, look for connections or contacts within your network that can be connected to them.

Identify Key Decision Makers – Generate a list of key people within the target organization that you would want to contact to discuss your value proposition.

Minimize Cold Calling by Prospecting through your Network – Look at whom your primary contacts are connected to. See if they have connections that you would like to meet. Keep this relationship oriented and don't abuse it.

Company Intelligence – Read through the profiles of leaders at companies you want to prospect with. Learn about the key initiatives they have achieved and possibly identify key selling "points of pain."

Target Market Research – Use LinkedIn to research the background and career experience of your customer. Helps you properly prepare for your selling process.

By no means are these the only tips that you should be aware of. Please feel free to share your tips at:
http://linktoprosper.com/Tips

14 Find and Be Found

People need social interaction. LinkedIn provides that but more importantly, it opens the door to business interaction.

With the proliferation of online social networks, both online and offline businesses have better potential for growth and networking. Due to that broad potential, the social networks themselves are making significant dollars. LinkedIn, which notes that they are profitable, hopes to generate $100 million in revenue in 2008 from a mix of advertising and fees. By comparison, MySpace, which is significantly larger, has been estimated to be grossing $800 million and Facebook about $300 million. So given all this "potential," we looked at ten possible ways to tap into this "potential."

Most online social networking sites tend to be merely for friendship. LinkedIn is more than that. Millions of registered users and businesses are using LinkedIn. This includes all of the Fortune 500 as well as famous people like John McCain, Barack Obama, T. Boone Pickens, Bill Gates and many more. In addition, there are over 150 industries that are represented in LinkedIn.

Given this broad spectrum of users, we based our list on the simple premise that LinkedIn is a place to be "found" or "find people" and through that philosophy, began to expand it out.

1. **Find & Follow "Thought Leaders"** – focus on your particular industry or keep it broad and look for some well known "gurus."

2. **Increase your Credibility** – use it like reality TV—have people follow your significant business moves through the "what are you working on now function."

3. **Increase your Web Traffic** – use LinkedIn to drive traffic to your blogs, websites, etc.

4. **Be an Idea Generator** – use LinkedIn Answers to get ideas for articles and posts to your own blog.

5. **Informal Advisory Board** – use LinkedIn Answers to tap into a variety of experts to answer your questions for free. It can be a great means of exchanging experience and business savvy.

6. **Enhance your Brand** – it's about giving more than you are getting.

7. **Competitive Intelligence** – follow your competition, determine the internal corporate structure of a competitor, review the company culture—i.e. turnover rates, promotion, and operational relationships, both internal & external.

8. **Industry Intelligence** – learn what others in your market are focused on.

9. **A Network of Support and Community** – small businesses sometimes lack this, especially with solopreneurs. With the coming of LinkedIn, small business owners can readily interact with others who have similar experience to their own. Who knows, business owners just might find angel investors willing to fund their ventures within the LinkedIn community!

10. **Locate Industry Experts Quickly** – the LinkedIn Advance Search page allows you to tap into a rich list of experts on almost every topic, industry or company. This is very important when you are looking for a critical skill set or much needed market research.

11. **Bonus** – target key employees that you may want to hire away from your competition.

People need social interaction. LinkedIn provides that but, more important, it opens the door to business interactions. We offer our short list of ways to tap into the potential this offers. However, our list is merely a drop in the bucket. Depending on your use of LinkedIn, there are many more ways that you can, and will, tap into. Remember the only limit to one's vision, is one's vision.

15 Think Outside the Box

Great business people who make business decisions have the knack for making great business decisions in a timely manner.

Great business people who make business decisions have the knack for making great business decisions in a timely manner. Perhaps that is something they are born with but, for sure, it is also based on the business support tools they have. LinkedIn should be one of these support tools as they have the capability of providing relevant information rapidly that can be used to assist in hiring, increasing sales and enabling more effective uses of business relationships.

Here's a rapid fire look at the potential LinkedIn offers businesses: research prospective partners, find industry experts, locate and get background information on potential employees, perform research on competitors, contact media, close sales rapidly with much less effort than traditional channels, etc., all of which can greatly improve your business.

Hiring Top Talent – great companies are built around top-tiered people and top-tiered people usually associate with other top-tiered people. So how can those relationships be effectively leveraged?

Apply LinkedIn to... leverage your employees' networks to find even more high quality talent. The most talented employees in any field are usually not looking for work because they are already employed. What better way to gain access to them than through a referral from one of your trusted employees?

More effective evaluation of Human Capital – the typical hiring process begins with the interview and then proceeds to a background check. Wouldn't it be more effective to vet all your applicant's references before you have an interview?

Apply LinkedIn to... view your applicants' profiles and verify all their references before your first meeting. Taking this to another level, think of the due diligence that can be performed using this process when considering the talent evaluation of a target company prior to the actual acquisition of that company. This alone could be worth millions.

Speaking engagements – these can be very powerful ways to reach your business partners, prospects or customers. However not all invitations to speak will result in getting your business in front of the proper audience.

Apply LinkedIn to... quickly check out the group to find out if they are legitimate and would be valuable for your company. Use a LinkedIn search to determine if you have any common contacts who you can contact to learn more about the group. Based on this research, you can quickly determine if it makes sense for you to commit.

These are but three specific applications of how LinkedIn can help your business. When used strategically, LinkedIn gives you a much deeper reach into your industry, the ability to access much greater talent, which in the end gives you greater knowledge that produces better results.

By having your team connected to LinkedIn, you can use each other's network as well as connect with your team. As we wrap up this rule, let's leave you with one more example of applying LinkedIn to a business scenario:

Suppose one of your sales people is calling on a new account and, in searching this company, they see that one of your connections knows the President of this new account. They now have the potential to leverage that connection chain to build a relationship with the new customer. This could result in a much quicker sales cycle and accelerate your business.

Section III
The LinkedIn Profile

GOAL: Determine the most effective way to communicate your brand and your value through the LinkedIn profile.

16 Understand Your LinkedIn Profile

LinkedIn claims that users with complete profiles are 40 times more likely to receive opportunities on LinkedIn.

If you're looking for new business opportunities or if you're looking to grow your career, LinkedIn is the place to be. LinkedIn offers you the opportunity to connect with tens of millions of professionals located throughout the world, which can help you to accomplish many of your professional goals.

It's a great place to find a job, seek a reference, hire a new employee, find an expert to interview, or just to network with others in your industry. You can connect with friends, colleagues and classmates from high school or college. With the Question and Answer feature, you can showcase your background and expertise by answering the questions of others from over 20 categories.

Completing Your Profile

LinkedIn claims that users with complete profiles are 40 times more likely to receive opportunities on LinkedIn. To help you develop out your Profile, LinkedIn provides a completeness scale for you. For instance, you may have noticed a little text blurb that states "Your Profile is 85% Complete." If you were ever wondering what attributes constitute a complete profile, they are:

- Entering your current position
- Filling in two past positions
- Providing your education history
- Adding your profile summary
- Uploading a profile photo

- Adding your specialties (which is also a great SEO tool)
- Gathering at least three recommendations

Updating & Revising Your Profile

Whenever you make changes to your profile, you need to select the edit link (which is either to the right or left) for EACH of the major categories on your profile (i.e. summary, education, etc.) and then follow the directions.

You may be aware that when you make a substantial change to your profile (for example by adding a new current job or school or website, etc.), your entire network receives an alert. You can control whether your connections receive updates. This is done by navigating to Profile Updates on the Account & Settings page.

Other Elements of the Profile

The Featured Logo – If a user has the "In" icon, they have premium accounts. Users with this icon showing may become *Featured* during searches if they most closely match the search criteria.

Thus...

Premium Account leads to "In" Icon...

...and

"In" displayed + most accurate search result = **Featured**

Status – If you are looking for a simple, yet non-intrusive way of communicating with your network, the Status function is the perfect tool. This tool allows you to share information regarding your current focus. When you choose to use the "What you are working on?" feature to enter a description, a status update is triggered and sent to your connection's home pages.

Your Photograph – A picture is worth a thousand words—or so they say. Adding your photograph to LinkedIn allows you to create another connection with anyone visiting your profile. A nice, professional headshot is the best choice, but any professional-looking photograph will do. When you add a photo it shows a different level of commitment to using the LinkedIn tool. Given the fact that we're visually oriented, adding anything that enhances your profile is a definite plus.

You have complete control over who sees your photo on LinkedIn. In fact, you have access to three levels of privacy. You can allow your direct connections, your network, or everyone access to your photo.

17 Give Yourself a Fast, Powerful Makeover!

Updating your professional headline is something that offers an incredible ROI in terms of benefit gained vs. time spent.

For most people, their LinkedIn experience begins with an invitation from someone they know. It is probably the curiosity factor that gets them to initially register with LinkedIn. We actually took a little non-scientific survey and that was what was overwhelmingly indicated as the impetus for registering.

While curiosity is an impetus, it is not one that is overwhelming. Thus people tend to go through the signup process as quickly as possible, usually not completely filling out their profile as no one likes to spend unnecessary time signing up on another one of these ubiquitous websites. Unfortunately, by racing through this, they also tend to overlook one of the most important elements to their LinkedIn success. During the registration process, one of the very first things someone needs to do is to create their professional headline. It may be subtle, but it is important, yet most people quickly skip past it addressing it only with the bare minimal requirement.

Think about this. Do you realize that every time your name appears on LinkedIn, your professional headline also appears? Your name could come up in a search or within someone's network or in the Outlook toolbar, but the bottom line is that everywhere your name comes up, so does your professional headline.

Essentially, this headline functions as your 3-second brand statement or your 3-second bumper sticker. Let's illustrate the power of this with a little example... which of these headlines is more powerful?

John Doe – 20 year expert facilitating $100,000,000 in High Tech Mergers

or

Bob Doe – Owner, Doe & Associates

Clearly, the first professional headline is more functional and quickly enables you to understand what John Doe does and where his key strength lies.

Now let's look at a practical implication of the two headlines above. Let's say you are doing a search on High Tech Mergers. Assume both John Doe and Bob Doe have the right keywords in their profile and they alone show up in the search. When you look at the search results, all you are able to see is a name and the professional description. Think about it, who are you going to be drawn to in a list of names, John or Bob Doe? It is very likely you will at least check out John because he tells you he is an expert in High Tech Mergers while Bob doesn't tell you anything of relevance.

We were speaking to a group of "C Level" business people discussing the value of a LinkedIn profile. To illustrate this point, we presented an individual's profile piecemeal. First, we highlighted his 300+ connections. Next we showed his vanity link, which made it easy to find his profile. Following this, we showed his links directing traffic to his blog and website. Then we asked, "Is this a maximized profile?" Most heads nodded yes. So... we finally showed his professional description, which was very vague and bland and asked if anyone in the room knew what this individual did. Since it was so nondescript, no one understood what this individual's expertise was. Now we asked again, "Was this a maximized profile?" This time, the answer was a resounding NO. The moral of the story is "Activity is not achievement." In this age of multi-tasking and business at the speed of light, no matter how many people you connect with, if people can't quickly ascertain your business value, the odds of them seeking to do business with you rapidly diminishes.

While we call it a 30-second makeover, whatever it takes you to do, is absolutely worth the investment of your time. Updating your professional headline is something that offers an incredible ROI in terms of benefit gained vs. time spent. Invest in yourself and quickly show the world your expertise and project your brand!

18 You Are Your Brand

Each of us projects our brand through everything we do, wear, touch or discuss.

There are millions and millions of registered users on LinkedIn. Given that sheer volume, how are you going to get people to find you and more importantly, when they do find you, are you projecting the right brand that will help your chances for success?

Let's start by asking *what is your brand*? Whether we acknowledge it or not, each of us projects our brand through everything we do, wear, touch or discuss. Therefore as many famous marketers have said, "You are Your Brand." We've compiled a list of things you can do to enhance your brand and improve your ability to get "found" on LinkedIn.

- Become a Thought Leader and find new relevant content that relates to your brand.
- Search on Google and Technorati for stories.
- Do a weekly scan of YouTube and the podcasts on iTunes to see if there are any new ones relevant to your brand.
- Convert your new, relevant information into a thought provoking question on LinkedIn Answers.
- Conversely, use some of that information to provide well thought through answers to LinkedIn questions.
- Consider using this "fresh content" to set up your own blog and offer key insights into your expertise.
- With your blog, use an easy-to-remember, content-appropriate domain name for your brand.

- Register your site with all the top search engines.
- Link your blog back to your LinkedIn profile.
- Use a specific name, relevant to your brand to name this link (i.e. Operations Guru.com vs. My Blog).
- Utilize the "what are you doing" function on your LinkedIn Profile but note only relevant things to your brand (not inconsequential ones).
- Along with your name, LinkedIn provides you with a small area to describe yourself. This is your "3-second pitch"—it is displayed every time your name comes up. Make sure you communicate your brand in this 8–10 word area. For instance, replace "Owner Video Corp" with "Video Expert providing cost-effective solutions to XYZ-type clients."
- Add your LinkedIn vanity URL to your email signature and business card
- LinkedIn allows you to email up to 200 people at a time—at some reasonable interval and when the information is relevant to your connections, communicate this information.
- When you invite someone to get LinkedIn to you, personalize the note.
- Provide LinkedIn recommendations to people whom you know very well. People appreciate these very much and this usually turns into something that will get returned to you.
- If you are networking in person, be aware of your clothes and appearance. They reflect your brand.
- Don't seek business opportunities right off. Instead, seek areas of shared interest and build a relationship.
- Try to always ask someone if there is something that you can do for them.
- Prepare ahead of time and read the blogs or check out the websites of key people that you communicate with.
- Don't lie, don't pitch and don't spam. Your brand should be that of providing value, not snake oil.
- (Bonus) Be Confident!

There are probably a bunch more tips to add, and we welcome them all. Feel free to share this list or leave comments with your own tips at http://linktoprosper.com/branding. All the best to developing your future success stories!

Promote Your Profile

Your profile is a billboard for you.

Your LinkedIn Profile is *Your Brand...* and it is the starting point of your LinkedIn experience. It is one of your most important elements on LinkedIn.

It's the place where you will summarize all of your professional endeavors including your employment, your website, your awards, certifications, background information, education and interests. It's also where you can post your photograph, adding another way to connect with others. Your profile is visible to the people who are included in your network—the people with whom you've directly connected. You should consider it a work in progress as you continually update it to increase its effectiveness.

Your Profile is a Billboard for You

Think of your profile like a billboard; you never know who is going to see it but for those who do read it, you want it to be as effective as possible.

LinkedIn actually lets you know who has read your profile. Have you ever noticed that little text box on the right side of your LinkedIn Home page that states, "*Your profile has been viewed by 103 people in the last 28 days. In the last 5 days you have appeared in search results 89 times?*"

If you haven't, that might mean one of two things:

- Since that feature is in LinkedIn beta testing, it might not always be available.

- Otherwise, more important, fewer than five people viewed your site in the last 30 days.

If you answered "b," then you really need to focus on attracting people to your profile, which can be done relatively easily.

Promoting Your Profile

A very simple and quick way to promote your profile is to create a vanity link and add it to your email signature. Perhaps do something like this—Want to connect with me on LinkedIn? Please visit http://linkedin.com/in/JohnDoe

Another straightforward way to promote your profile is accomplished simply through inviting more people to connect. Once they receive the invitation, they can accept and then view your profile.

An additional way to promote your profile is to use HTML logos and links on your blogs and internet sites.

A broader way to promote your profile relates to the search engines. Currently public profiles on LinkedIn are being indexed in the major search engines. Thus limited information from your profile can show up on a Google search, if you set your public profile preferences to display the sections of your LinkedIn profile that you want non-LinkedIn users to see. This information is limited to only your name, title, industry, metropolitan area, number of connections, and number of recommenders. To contact with you, any of these viewers would have to go through and follow officially LinkedIn sanctioned channels. You can always edit this function on the Settings Page and clicking on My Public Profile.

So Who Can View My Profile?

As we've seen, people who aren't on LinkedIn can view a subset of your profile if you so choose. Registered users on LinkedIn, who are within your 3-degree network, can see your name and full profile. In addition, certain premium corporate subscribers can see the same information if you allow those views. Everyone else outside your network will only see a limited view of your profile.

20 | Personalize Your Profile

Accessing Your Profile: Creating a Personal URL

Wouldn't it be great to have a professional looking URL for your LinkedIn profile that would be easy to communicate verbally or would look great on your business card, website or other marketing collateral? Well, now you can.

When you create a LinkedIn profile, a link is automatically created for you that includes the LinkedIn domain name followed by a stream of random letters and numbers—definitely not easy to remember and certainly not attractive. This link is what takes someone directly to your LinkedIn profile.

An attractive feature of LinkedIn is that you can personalize this URL using your name (if it's not already taken) or other identifying words, such as the name of your company. For example, Albert Einstein might have created a personal LinkedIn URL that looked like this:
http://LinkedIn.com/in/AlbertEinstein

You can create your personal URL by clicking on Account & Settings at the top of your LinkedIn page. Next, go to Profile Settings, click on Public Profile and you'll be taken to another screen. At the top you'll be able to edit your Public Profile. Now you can add your personal URL to anything you want.

Keep in mind that someone else may have already reserved your name—because many people have the same name. If yours is taken, you might try adding an initial or a title or a suffix (Mr./Ms., Doctor, MD, PhD, etc.). Alternatively, you can add the name of your business. Also, keep in mind that your personal URL must include at least five letters.

Your Profile and LinkedIn Groups

Groups are communities within LinkedIn where you can connect with others who share similar affiliations by industry, association, company, or some other common connection. When you join a LinkedIn group, your profile becomes visible to all of the group members.

Keep in mind, however, that group members cannot see your network of connections unless you make them visible to them or unless you are personally connected to that particular group member.

Remember you can control if others can view your connections by going to Account & Settings, Settings, Privacy Settings, and then clicking on Connections Browse. You can control whether or not your connections are able to view the people you are connected to, although they will always be able to see shared connections.

Adding Connections but without Alerting My Network

The default on LinkedIn is to allow your connections to be notified whenever you add a new one. If you prefer not to alert everyone (and prevent your connections from seeing each other in your network) you can adjust this on the Account & Settings page. Once on the page, under Privacy Settings, click on Connection Browse. Select "No" for the questions, "Allow your connections to view the rest of your connections list?" Then save your changes.

My Photo Disappeared? What Now?

Did you upload a photo but now you find that it's missing from your LinkedIn profile? It may have been removed because it was flagged by another user or LinkedIn management as inappropriate. As a professional networking site, LinkedIn requires that you must use a photo to which you own the rights. That is, you cannot use copyrighted photos even if they are of you! You must own the copyright to your material.

Also, it must be a picture of you and not someone or something else. As a professional site, you're not allowed to use images of scenery, animals, designs, or anything of the like. You can change or update your photograph at any time, however, by following the simple upload instructions.

Section IV
Building Your
Network

GOAL: Generate efficient strategies that enable you to build an effective network.

Lay the Foundation for Your Network

Quality matters here. Fifty quality contacts are infinitely more valuable to you than 500 people you really don't communicate with.

LinkedIn says "it's not about connections for connection's sake" and we agree.

First, decide whom you want to invite. Quality matters here. 50 quality contacts are infinitely more valuable to you than 500 people you really don't communicate with. The quality of your network should not be measured numerically. Instead, it should be measured by the number and quality of the resources available from your network.

3 Degrees of Separation

LinkedIn functions in a very similar way to the old "6 degrees of Kevin Bacon" game, in which any actor can be linked through their film role to Kevin Bacon. The main difference is that LinkedIn focuses on three levels of connections.

Assume you are like the sun and the center of your network universe. Directly connected to you are your 1st degree connections. These are your "hot connections." The people directly connected to your 1st degree connections are your 2nd degree connections. These are sort of your "warm connections." Finally, the direct connections of your 2nd degree connections are your 3rd degree connections. These can be considered your "cool connections."

My Contacts

Your 1st degree or direct connections offer the ability to:

* View or browse profiles
* Have direct contact via email
* Forward Introductions to people who aren't directly connected to the intended recipient
* View information regarding my contacts (this is set by default but can be adjusted in the Account & Settings page)

Your 2nd & 3rd degree connections obviously are more removed and offer very little free "direct" contact.

Your Strategy

In one of the first rules in this book, you were asked the question, "Why are you on LinkedIn?" and "What are looking to achieve?" Your answers to those questions should help you build out your network foundation. Let's say that you determine your goals for using LinkedIn are to meet potential future employers within the new media space. Given the three degrees of separation, it is almost a guarantee that you have the potential to connect with some very important influencers in that space. So with the direction you choose, begin to build your network with people you know who can connect you to others within that business vertical. You don't need to strictly adhere to this by limiting everyone else from connecting to you, but you should be prioritizing how to find the right "connections."

It Takes Effort

We will touch on this in greater detail in another rule, but it bears mentioning here too. You get what you give on LinkedIn. If you don't try to connect with people who can help you achieve your goal, you won't. We know one example of someone who kept trying to connect individually with people in a specific business vertical but, for some reason, it just wasn't working. He decided to take another approach and set up his own group, which actually helped him become a well-connected person within his business niche. The key takeaway here is to keep trying if your efforts don't immediately pay off.

22

Use Invitations to Connect

Let's start with the basics. Each registered user builds their network on LinkedIn via "connections." Thus if you have 55 connections, you have 55 people whom you've either invited to be part of your network or vice versa.

Keeping with the basics for a moment longer, for two people to "connect," one must invite the other and the other must accept. If the person being invited is already on LinkedIn, all they need to do is accept the invite. If the person is not on LinkedIn, they will need to register in order to accept the invitation.

The most basic way for people to build their network is to start with their personal contact lists. People in these lists might include someone you have worked with, collaborated on projects with or maybe attended school with.

To add people to your network, you can invite them one at a time and enter their email address into the Quick Invite box or Add Connections button. If you are a brand new user, this is recommended, so that you can begin to get an understanding for how the process works. You will need to know their First and Last Names as well as their email addresses.

Invite Connections Already On LinkedIn

For a quicker method, you can quickly see which of your contacts are already on LinkedIn and invite them en masse. You can upload your contacts from Outlook or upload a .CSV file of your contacts into the "Other Contacts" section of your LinkedIn account.

Using LinkedIn's Colleague and Classmate Reconnect

Colleague Reconnect enables you to find current LinkedIn users whom you may have worked with in the past or may currently be working with. Similarly, Classmate Reconnect enables you to find current LinkedIn users who were (or currently are) classmates of yours.

In both cases, LinkedIn searches users experiences that match yours (i.e. same employer, same college, etc.) and the displays the results which enables you to decide who you may want to connect with.

Using the LinkedIn Outlook Toolbar

This is a tool that is both efficient and effective. Among other things, for every email you receive, this tool enables you to check the LinkedIn status of the sender. A major benefit of this tool is that it can identify people who:

- you normally communicate with
- are on LinkedIn
- may have been overlooked in all the other ways you have of adding connections

This icon is located in the top right corner of every email. Simply mouse over it to check a person's status.

LinkedIn Grab

In addition, the LinkedIn Toolbar has a feature called "Grab," which allows you to "grab" someone's email signature and automatically add it to your Outlook Contacts.

Sending Invitations Directly from Outlook

The Toolbar also provides a "Dashboard" function. There is a section within this function labeled "Contacts to Invite." You can click the invite link which will invite people to join your network right from there without you having to login to LinkedIn. You are also able to personalize the message you want to send.

Withdrawing an Invitation

If after sending an invitation, you want to withdraw it, simply go back to the invite and click the withdraw button.

23 Understand Invitation Etiquette

Receiving, accepting & limiting invitations.

When you go to a party, arrive for a business meeting or play golf, you generally follow a certain etiquette for the proper way to interact. For the most part, people want to do what is socially approved and to this regard there are various books that teach them. However instead of offering a book, we'll offer a rule on LinkedIn invitation etiquette.

Receiving Invitations

Upon receipt of an invitation you can do any of the following:

- Accept the Invite
- Or... If you don't know the user, you can:
  - *Do Nothing* – Invitations typically expire after a few weeks. If no action is taken, you will receive reminders that you have an outstanding invitation. If an invitation does expire, assuming the person is very interested in connecting with you, they will still have the opportunity to resend you an invitation.
  - *Click "decide later"* which will archive the message and prevent the member from sending you another invitation at a later time. This, along with the next two options, will prevent any future reminders from coming to you.

- **You can use the "Reply" link and send a message back to the inviter.** LinkedIn offers the following as an example, *Thank you for the invitation to connect however I'm afraid I cannot accept it at this time. LinkedIn is a powerful tool for managing my professional network and designed to help me maintain the connections I have. It is a LinkedIn best practice to only connect directly to those whom I know well and would recommend. I'd like to be able to give a referral to any of my connections when asked. If I don't know you well enough to do so, LinkedIn isn't as powerful for my network. Please understand and remember to invite me to connect after we've had a chance to work together.*

- **Click the "I don't know" button.** While this prevents the sender from sending you another invite, it may also place a mark on the sender's account that tells LinkedIn this person may not be using invitations correctly.

Accepting My Invitations

You can tell when someone accepts your invitation a couple of ways.

- You receive an email with the acceptance
- You can see your status change on your home page

You can view the status of your invitation from your LinkedIn Inbox.

Limiting Invitations

As mentioned previously, the goal of LinkedIn is not to gather connections for connections' sake. Instead, it is to build out a quality network.

In the process of doing this, you may find that you want to limit the type of people who can connect with you. For instance, if you have been receiving, or simply don't want to receive invites from people you don't know, you can turn on LinkedIn's invitation filtering feature. The basic effect of this is to allow you to create a "white list" of people that are only found in your uploaded address book.

Since LinkedIn notifies you of all incoming invitations by default, you will need to adjust this setting.

If you select the "Only notify me of invitations from people in my 'Other Contacts' list" option, invitations sent to you will not appear in your email inbox but will be diverted to a "Blocked Invitations" page. If you want, you can check these whenever you'd like.

24 Add People to Your Network

Building your network is all about effort. The more time and effort you put in, the greater the value of your network.

If we received a penny every time we heard people complaining that they weren't really successful in building out their network (yet never really put in any effort), we might have enough money to buy a cup of coffee at Starbucks. All joking aside, building a quality network is going to require effort. Anybody that says differently is trying to sell air.

We are not advocating spending hours on this but we are looking to identify time effective ways for you to increase the quality of your LinkedIn network. Let's start by taking a look at the easiest ways to grow your network and then progress to those that take a little more effort

"Contacts 101" – It is to your benefit to approach this strategically and make a list of the people you know well (friend, family, co-workers), and then invite them to link in. "Dig" into your past when filling in your profile. The more you include, the better your chances of being found by people you've previously associated with. In your profile include past companies, education, affiliations, activities, etc.

Utilizing the *People You May Know Function* – LinkedIn provides a list of suggestions for people whom you may know but not yet be connected to. This is located in the upper right corner of your Home page. The information that populates this list is generated during the uploading of your contacts. LinkedIn counts the number of emails sent to a particular person and this is used to determine whom you may want to invite.

A Customized Email Signature – Another simple yet subtle way for you to efficiently connect with people is through adding a link in your email signatures. To help facilitate this, LinkedIn offers a customized email signature for Microsoft Outlook. Actually, they offer 15+ types of designs. Recipients whose email settings do not allow HTML email will not see the signature included with your message.

Non-Customized Email Signature – There is a pretty simple and low tech way to get someone to learn more about you and possibly connect with you. Use a vanity link in your email signature. This would look something like this http://LinkedIn.com/in/JohnDoe. It shows up in all emails and is a passive way to get people to see all your credentials.

Groups – The jury is still out on the value of them but, at the very least, you have the opportunity to connect with people who have similar interests. We've made some interesting connections this way.

Answers – Ask and answer questions. It is a great way to promote yourself. Generally expect to make a couple of connections through each activity, however we have heard about people that get 10 or more new connections through their Q&A.

Consider becoming a LION – A LION is a LinkedIn Open Networker, meaning that you agree to accept all invitations. The phrase is included in your profile and thus searchable. People seek out LIONs during searches to increase their network. If quantity is what you are after, this is a relatively simple and time effective way to generate connections.

SEO Yourself – Use your profile link in various places on the web like blog comments, etc. This is another simple tactic that will also help to improve your Google page rank.

25 Don't Abuse Introductions and InMails

Focus on building out your network with quality introductions; seeking connections for connections' sake is garbage in/garbage out.

Having the ability to tap into contacts of your contacts is obviously very powerful. Thus you should consider ways of leveraging your contacts to get introduced to their con-tacts—keep in mind however that this is a rela-tionship, and don't abuse it.

Introductions

One way to expand your network is to browse the connections of your direct connections. This will enable you to potentially find people whom your direct connections know and you would like to be introduced to.

Hence, LinkedIn offers its Introduction feature. This is one way to *contact* people in your network. To be clear on terminology here, *con-nections* are made through invitations, not through Introductions.

Let's assume that you want to connect with someone who is two degrees away from you. You would contact a direct connection for both you and that person. Then you would ask this direct connect to forward an Introduction. It is up to them as to whether they will forward it. This is another example of where a "quality" network is more valuable than a "quantity" network. The better you know this direct connection, the higher the likelihood that they will make the introduction for you.

To be most effective, LinkedIn introductions should *only be used with 2nd degree members*. In this manner, you will know everyone who may see your request.

Also, when reaching out to another member via an Introduction, ensure that you review that member's profile closely and determine what type of contact they are open to.

Depending on your membership, you will have between 5 and 25 introductions you can use per month. You can always tell how many you have left by going to your Account & Settings page.

InMail

This is another way to contact any user directly on LinkedIn. However you need to purchase these. InMails are private messages that enable users to contact each other with LinkedIn acting as the intermediary to ensure that all messages remain confidential and that contact information is kept private. If the recipient is not in your network, you will only see the recipient's name and email address if the InMail message is accepted.

InMails can be purchased individually or as part of a premium account. Since senders pay for each InMail sent, they tend to choose the people they contact with care. If you use them, understand that, once they are sent, they expire within 15 days if not read by the receiver. This is free when contacting an Open Network Member.

InMail Feedback

This is a reputation system LinkedIn uses to minimize spam. It is based on recipients' responses to senders' InMail messages. In general, you are notified only when InMails come from senders with a 3-star rating or higher. You can change your preferences in your Contact Settings. As with Introductions, you can always tell how many you have left by going to your Account & Settings page.

People like to talk about how their network connects them to over 1 million people. With these tools you begin to tap into and leverage these connections.

26 Manage Your Connections

Failing to manage your connections is akin to asking someone out on a date but never showing up.

As we've been highlighting, one important goal of your LinkedIn experience is to build out a network of quality contacts. Thus, as it develops, you will naturally need to manage it. This will range from simple managing of views to removing connections you no longer need. Here are some things you should be aware of.

Sorting Connections – As you add new connections to your network, they are aggregated in one location and the only way to sort through them is alphabetically. We know that many people want to sort them in a variety of ways including by function or by how well you know the connection, etc. While LinkedIn does not allow you to do this on the site, it does provide an export function, which enables you to export your connections in a .CSV format, which can then be easily loaded into Excel. From there you will be able to sort, rank, prioritize and group your connections exactly as you want to.

Missing Connections – Have you ever logged on but couldn't find a connection you know you've already added? This occurs because you've set up multiple accounts while accepting an invitation to connect. It happens quite a bit actually, or at least it happens quite a bit to people whom we are connected to. To remedy this, you will need to transfer your contacts and close the duplicate account.

Managing the Way Your Network Views Your Connections – By default, your direct connections are able to browse through the connections of all the other people in your network. If you want to prevent anyone from viewing the connections in your network, you can do the following:

- Click on the Account & Settings button.
- On the Settings page, under Privacy Settings, click on the text link for Connections Browse.
- Under Connections Browse, select "No, hide my connections list."

Removing Imported Contacts – If you find that some of your imported contacts are no longer valid, the easiest way to remove them is by reloading your most current contact list.

Removal of a Connection from Your List – For a variety of reasons you may find yourself wanting to remove a connection from your list. This is pretty simple to do.

- Start by going to My Contacts.
- Click Remove Connections.
- Highlight the Connections to Remove.
- Select the Remove Connections Button.

On a side note, if you want to remove a connection, the removal is neither captured in any alert nor is the other member notified. Once removed, they cannot be re-added.

Repairing a Disconnection to a Previous Connection

You may have disconnected to a prior network connection for any number of reasons. If you now want to reconnect with this person, you have two alternatives. One option is to invite the individual back to your network, but you'll need to use a different email address for them. The other alternative is to have that member send you an invitation so you can reconnect with them. While this might not happen too often, it's always good to know how to "repair" a disconnection.

Good News to Report? Share it with Your Network

Do you want to share some news with your connections? Just go to your Inbox and select Compose Message. You'll be able to select who receives your message.Your connections will receive a message in their LinkedIn email that you've sent them a new message.

Section V
Recommendations and Answers

GOAL: Learn about some of the most powerful tools that LinkedIn offers to demonstrate your expertise.

Manage Your Recommendations

Recommendations are a part of relationship building, which can lead to all sorts of things including new customers, business partners, or even a new job.

Everyone likes to be recognized for their achievements and LinkedIn provides a function called Recommendations that facilitates just that. LinkedIn's Recommendation feature enables people that know you the best to publicly praise you. Clearly, adding Recommendations to your profile should increase the credibility you want to exude. Also, without three recommendations, any LinkedIn profile is not complete.

People like to do business with people they know, like and trust and LinkedIn states that "Users with recommendations in their profiles are three times more likely to receive relevant offers and inquiries through searches on LinkedIn."

There are a variety of ways to ask for recommendations. LinkedIn even provides a template located on the Request Recommendation page that allows you to request a recommendation.

When seeking a Recommendation, base your decision on people who know you the best and value your work. LinkedIn recommends:

- Former managers
- Colleagues and co-workers
- Customers and clients
- Business partners

Recommendations are a part of relationship building, which can lead to all sorts of things including new customers, business partners, or even a new job. Be generous and genuine with recommending others and also don't be shy about asking for recommendations in return.

As you receive more and more recommendations, you may ultimately need to manage them. Whether you request a recommendation or receive one that was unsolicited, you will be alerted to them in the same manner through a LinkedIn email message. These are always exciting to receive. Once you approve the recommendation, it will appear on your Profile. In addition, an alert will go out to your network telling them that you have just been recommended.

You have something called a "Received Recommendations Summary Page." From this page, you will be able to manage all the recommendations you have received by position and whether you want them displayed on your profile.

Editing a Recommendation – You have complete control over the recommendations you receive, meaning that you are able to revise, replace or withdraw any recommendation.

Moving Recommendation – Sometimes the recommendation you receive may not apply to the position you feel it is most associated with. If you want to have it moved to another position, you will need to contact the sender and have them make the change on their side, withdraw the original and resend the revised recommendation. This is certainly not the most difficult process, but due to the logistics required, probably not one that you want to pursue unless you feel very strongly about it.

Recommendations that Disappear – If you notice that a recommendation has disappeared, there are two possible reasons. First, the author of the recommendation may have withdrawn it, as they have the right to. If not, then the position associated with the recommendation has been removed and the recommendation is effectively unassigned. If you re-add the position, you can reapply the recommendation.

Point to Ponder – for those who want to keep their networks private, you need to keep your recommendations private too. If you allow them to be seen, you allow those that recommend you to be seen as well.

To add your tips on Recommendations, please feel free to go to
http://LinkToProsper.com/tips

28 | Make Recommendations

Recommendations provide a lot of value to you, the writer, and to your friend or colleague, the recipient

Recommendations provide a lot of value to you, the writer, and to your friend or colleague, the recipient. By acknowledging someone's great service, performance or other contributions, you'll create an even stronger relationship with them. An added bonus is that your name is also featured as part of the recommendation, so both parties can gain visibility.

What's even better is that LinkedIn has no limit to the number of recommendations you can make. So consider reviewing your LinkedIn network and make it a regular practice to write recommendations to acknowledge great performance. These will automatically become a part of the recipients' profiles should they accept your recommendations.

It's easy to leave a recommendation for someone. Click on their profile, then go to the upper right corner of their page and click the link Recommend this Person. Follow the instructions and you'll be on your way.

Things to consider in writing a Recommendation

Before making your first recommendation, a good suggestion would be to read others to get a feel for what to say and what not to say. Whenever you give a Recommendation, you need to keep in mind that these are professional, so keep away from cutesy terms or slang. Some people who struggle with finding the "right words" will be best served by getting "inspiration" from words that other people have used. A second point would be to be as specific as possible. This makes your Recommendation more credible. After all what is better—"Johnny is great because he works long hours," or "Johnny's dedication to the team was clearly observed in his coming in numerous days at 4 AM to support the European team before the rest of the company arrived for work." Lastly, shorter is better—conciseness and clarity rule here. Also, follow up with the person you recommended to see how they like it and let them know you would be willing to edit it if you missed something important.

Making a Recommendation

There are three ways in which you can create a recommendation for another registered user. You can do it from your profile, from their profile or in response to their request for a recommendation.

The process of providing a recommendation is pretty consistent across these three methods. Essentially, you name the person to be recommended, describe the capacity in which you will be doing the recommendation—colleague (worked at same company), service provider (you've hired them before), business partner (you've worked with them but not as a colleague or service provider) or student. Then you are ready to write your recommendation.

Withdrawing a Recommendation

Sometimes situations change and you may find that you are no longer able to provide a recommendation that you once gave. As the author of a recommendation, you have the ability to withdraw your recommendation but once you withdraw it, it is permanently removed. Please note that the recipient will not be notified. To withdraw, you would need to go to "Manage Your Recommendations," select the recommendation you want to remove and click "Withdraw this Recommendation."

29 Ask a Question

Asking questions on LinkedIn is like having your own personal board of directors... without the expense!

One of the most relevant and powerful tools that LinkedIn offers is the LinkedIn Answers function. In its most basic form, it provides you with an instant informal board of advisors with an almost infinite knowledge base.

Do you have a question about something work-related? Are you working on a project and need to find resources (people, companies, sites, blogs, etc.) that might be helpful? Do you have a question about a company or industry? LinkedIn Answers is the place to go. Are you an expert or do you want to build up expert status? Consider perusing the daily questions posed by others and start answering them. This will allow others to benefit from your knowledge and possibly open up new networking opportunities.

How to Ask a Question

To access the LinkedIn Answers feature, go to the navigation bar located in the upper left corner of the page. Click on Answers and a drop-down box will appear. To post a question, select Ask a Question. You'll be taken to another page where you have several items to complete and selections to make.

Suggestions

First, write a succinct question. Keep it short and to the point. No rambling paragraphs or long sentences. If you want more people to read it and respond, keep your questions highly focused.

Your questions should be knowledge-based, not about connecting with other people. If you ask a question that enables someone to share their expertise, they will do that more freely. However, it is doubtful they will bother if you are only asking a question that is looking for them to connect you with someone else.

Please note that questions that simply ask for introductions etc., usually don't get answered but they do get flagged. If a question receives several flags, it is removed and users who have several flagged questions may lose the right to post any additional questions.

Once your question is written, you select whether or not you want people outside your network to see the question. Unless you have a geographically-specific question, it's probably better to allow anyone to respond, as this will probably result in more responses.

The next section in the asking question process labeled "Add Details" is optional. If you have more clarifying details or content to add, this is the place to do it. Again, try to bullet point your thoughts. Keep your sentences short and make sure you're only supplying relevant detail necessary for someone to best answer your question. You may want to have a friend or colleague review what you've written to make sure it's understandable.

Once you've completed this, you are asked to Categorize Your Question in one of 20+ business categories. After you select a category, you can further refine it by selecting a sub-category that best relates to the topic of your question.

You can then select geography as a further refinement if that is relevant to the information you're seeking. You can select by country or zip code. And, finally, you can categorize your question as to whether it relates to Recruiting, Promoting Your Services, or Job Seeking.

One final thought—communicating with people who have taken the time to answer your question is a great way to find kindred spirits and potentially add good, solid connections to your network.

30 Answer a Question

Answering questions provides a great avenue for you to meet and connect with others on LinkedIn who share your business interests.

Answering questions on LinkedIn is a fantastic feature that enables you to demonstrate your knowledge, enhance your credibility and is yet another way to connect with others—both inside and outside your network.

How to Answer a Question

Answering a question is just as straightforward as asking a question. Again, to access the LinkedIn Answers feature, go to the navigation bar located in the upper left corner of the page. Click on Answers and a drop-down box will appear. To answer questions, select Answer Questions.

You'll see a list of the most recently asked questions. You can review the open questions, or you can select questions from any of 20+ categories of questions by making a selection from the detailed menu located on the right side of the page. Again, you can click on any of these main categories to further refine your search for questions in a more detailed sub-category.

To answer a question, click on the question and a new page will open that displays the full question, along with any supplemental information that the author has included. Below the question, you'll notice two buttons—Answer and Suggest Expert. One allows you to respond to the question with your own answer while the other allows you to select someone from your network who might be a helpful resource.

If you click on Answer, you'll find areas to input your answer, note additional resources and even post a private message to the person posting the question. You'll also have the option, once again, to suggest an expert from your network.

Suggestions

LinkedIn provides the writer of the question the ability to judge the answers they receive, with the aptly named title—Best Answer. While it hasn't been conclusively shown that this offers dramatic value to your profile, it can be another feather in your cap that supports the building of your brand.

As with asking questions, take a little time to answer questions in a way that exhibits your expertise. Again, LinkedIn is a communication tool, and if you answer a question posed by someone you don't know, the first impression you are going to be offering about your brand is going to be based on your answer. Thus if the question were, "How should I create my target customer?" and one answer were, "I never really bother as I don't have a problem with it," vs. " I look at age, income, sex, marital status, geographic location, types of print media used, etc.," which would be a better way to express your brand? Clearly the second allows you to demonstrate your knowledge in a short yet thoughtful and knowledgeable manner.

Answering questions (along with asking questions) provides a great avenue for you to meet and connect with others on LinkedIn who share your business interests. Many times the author of the question will reach out to thank you for taking the time to respond. By doing this, the communication process between you and the author has started.

Lastly and most importantly, your answers can be found by Google. Read the entire question before answering and do your best to respond with the information that is sought by the individual who posted the question.

Section VI
Learning the "How-To" for Other LinkedIn Functions

GOAL: Learn specific tactics and step-by-step rules for using various LinkedIn functionalities.

31

Manage Your Account

The most important thing you need to consider is that your email address is your communication link with LinkedIn.

Although email is fairly routine, there are certain elements with the use of your email in LinkedIn that are a fairly important element of your LinkedIn experience. The most important thing you need to consider is that your email address is your communication link with LinkedIn. If you currently use your work email to access LinkedIn, be aware that if you lose access to that work account (by exiting the company) you will lose access to your LinkedIn communications.

Your Primary Email Account

You may consider using a non-work email account as your communication link to LinkedIn. If you need to change the primary email address, here's what you can do:

- Click the "Account & Settings" link.
- Select Email Address (found under Personal Information section).
- Click the Add Email Address button.
- Enter the new email address and click "Add Email Address."

After this you will receive a confirmation message with the new email address. Just follow the instructions to confirm this new email.

Eliminating Multiple Accounts/Closing Your Account

Many people have set up multiple accounts that they no longer use. These accounts can become confusing to people trying to find you, or provide an incomplete profile, thus hindering your branding capability. Also, if you opened multiple accounts and try to add an email address that is already on one of these accounts, you will receive an error message during this process.

To eliminate these excess accounts, we suggest the following steps:

- Transfer all your information (profile, connections etc.) to one account and close the other(s).

- You can close a LinkedIn account online by logging into the account you wish to close and then going to the Personal Information section in Account & Settings and selecting Close Your Account.

Once an account is closed, you lose access to the account and any information tied to that.

Transferring Your Contacts

If you have inadvertently set up multiple accounts, you'll want to move all of your contacts into one account by transferring them. The process for transferring is as follows:

- Open each "old" account.
- Click on My Contacts.
- At the bottom of My Contacts, click on the link to Export Connections.
- Select Microsoft Outlook (.CSV File), enter the security image and click Export.
- When the pop-up window opens, select Save to Disk then click on OK.
- Log in to your "new" account and click on Add Connections.
- Import your Contacts by following the instructions on the page.

At this point, all of your Contacts should now be uploaded.

Your Email Privacy

Are you concerned about who can view your primary email address? The answer is all of your direct connections. On the opposite side of privacy, some people post their email addresses in their LinkedIn profile.

32 Get Serious About Search

Search, search, search... those who search for connections on LinkedIn are greatly enhancing their chances of success.

Since there are millions of registered users on LinkedIn, and since the purpose of LinkedIn is to find people as well as to be found, learning how to use the Search Function is very important.

In LinkedIn there are a few different types of searches and, in this rule, we will walk you through them.

Profile Search Functions

Exact Phrases – If you are searching for a specific phrase, you must enclose the phrase in quotes (i.e. *"Investment Banking"*)

Excluding an element of a Phrase – If you want to do a search but want to exclude an element of a phrase, you must put a minus sign (a.k.a. a dash) immediately before that term (for example, -personal banking). In this example, the term "personal banking" will be excluded.

The "OR" Function – If you are searching for one of two (or more) phrases, you should separate the phrase with an upper case OR (e.g., *Director OR Manager*)

Multiple Phrases – If you are searching for two phrases within a profile, you should separate the phrase with an upper case AND (e.g., *Director AND Manager*). As an FYI, even if you don't include the AND, the search defaults to it (e.g., *Director Manager*).

Complex Searches – Since titles are not standard across companies, you may want to use similar phrases with inclusion and exclusion when searching. In these cases, you would use parentheses. For instance, a search like this, GM OR (VP AND Europe) would find people who have GM or VP AND Europe in their profiles.

Keyword Search Functions

Title – Search for users with a particular title. If you check "current titles only," only users who currently hold that title will be returned.

Company – Search for users at a particular company. Select "current companies only" to find only people who are currently at that company.

Keywords – Enter any keyword.

Industry – Searches for users in one or more primary industries. You can select multiple industries by holding the Ctrl (PC) or Command (Mac) buttons.

Location – Put in a zip code. This enables you to search not just that zip code, but the users in the surrounding metro area as well.

Reference Search Function

This type of search can help you find people in your network who could be references for prospective clients, business partners, and employees. One quick tip—if you didn't get many results, try to search on a less specific company name; for example, IBM as opposed to International Business Machines.

Name Search Function

The last of the three main search types is the Name Search Function. This enables you to search by Name (Last names only), Company (search for a particular company) or Location. This is pretty much duplicated by the main advanced search page.

Think About Upgrading

To upgrade or not to upgrade... the question is power.

By default, once you register on LinkedIn, you are given a free Personal Account. If you so choose, you can upgrade to a paid, "premium" account called Business or Business Plus. Essentially what you pay for is the ability to reach or be reached by the right people on LinkedIn.

Your Personal Account (Free)

Since this is the default account, this is the one that the vast majority of LinkedIn users have and, depending on what you want to achieve, may be the only account that you need. It enables you to do everything on LinkedIn like:

- Create a strong profile around your brand
- Search profiles of other LinkedIn users
- Provide links to your websites
- Invite people & build your network
- Ask and answer questions in LinkedIn Answers
- Join various LinkedIn Groups
- Provide and request recommendations
- Request up to 5 introductions at a time

In short, you have the ability to create a professional presence with a strong communication channel.

Premium Accounts (Paid)

LinkedIn offers a couple of Premium accounts that they believe offer better communication, more powerful search tools, and enhanced access to decision makers and other resources on LinkedIn.

If you think of these accounts in tiers, the first tier would be the free account and the second tier would be the Business Account. The latter costs $19.95 per month or $199.50 per year.

Going one step higher, there is a third tier of accounts called the Business Plus accounts. This type of account costs $50 per month or $500 per year.

Managing Your Account

On almost every page, you will see a text link to Account & Settings. This is the page that enables you to manage your account and control the environment you create for yourself on LinkedIn.

The "Account" section of this page is your dashboard to manage your account. This includes details such as your account type, start date, and summaries of Introductions and InMails available to you. In addition, if you are a subscriber, you will see information pertinent to that including your subscription end date, your OpenLink membership status and the number of job credits you have available.

Account Cancellation

If you want to cancel your premium membership, you need to go to the customer Service Center, select *Ask Customer Service* and submit your request.

Typically, your LinkedIn Account should be closed immediately but it can take up to 72 hours for your public profile to be removed. Any information residing on the web will continue to reside there until those sites update their information from LinkedIn. You may want to contact them if your information is not removed.

Manage Your Settings

Take control of your LinkedIn experience.

In LinkedIn, you manage all of your Account and Settings from a page appropriately called, Account & Settings. The page is split in two, with the top half of the page focused on your Account (which was covered in the previous rule).

The second half or the bottom portion of the Account & Settings page provides you insight into your LinkedIn Settings. These settings will control your privacy, your profile, your communication flow, etc. In short, they control your LinkedIn experience. The layout of these settings is fairly straightforward and is easy to navigate.

Profile Settings

In this section you can control:

- What appears in your LinkedIn Profile – this essentially links you to the edit function of your profile.
- Your Photo—pretty intuitive – controls what you show.
- Your Updates – which lets you control how you notify your connections of significant changes to your LinkedIn profile.
- Your Public Profile URL – which is the URL that someone can use to find your Profile.

- Manage your Recommendations – includes managing both the ones you've received as well as the ones you've sent. Links to pages where you can revise, replace, or withdraw specific recommendations you've made.

Receiving Messages

In this section, you can control your contacts to set the kinds of contacts you want to make, let users know you want to be contacted, and give potential contacts advice about approaching you, or let people know that you prefer to be left alone.

Other key elements of this section include managing your:

- Invitations – shows status and controls how you're notified when another user invites you to connect.

- Profile Updates – controls how you are notified of changes to your connections' profiles. To effectively tap into the benefits of passive communication, this is important.

- Email Updates – which allow you to control what new products and features exist from LinkedIn.

- Contact Settings – allows you to set the types of contact you are interested in.

Personal Information

This section enables you to control how your name and location are displayed. In addition, you control displaying your primary email address. You can change your password here and if necessary, close your account from this section as well.

Privacy Settings

Under the Privacy settings, you can control the following:

- Partner Sites – determine how your profile is displayed on sites that partner with LinkedIn.

- Connections Browse – allows you to determine whether or not your connections can view your connection list.

- Profile Views – when you visit someone's profile, you can determine what if anything is shown to the person you viewed.

- Profile & Status Update – you control what notifications are made when you make significant changes to your profile.

- Service Provider Directory – this is a listing of service providers that have received a recommendation.

35 Create Your Own LinkedIn Group

Setting up groups is fast, easy and a great way to connect with other like-minded LinkedIn members.

You can create a specialized community of like-minded folks who can interact and create even stronger networks among themselves. Not only can you invite folks from your own network, but you can also reach out and find others within the larger LinkedIn network who might enjoy being a part of your group. LinkedIn is the perfect place to feature your group and it's easy to set up and manage a group.

Starting a Group

If you want to start a new LinkedIn Group, simply log into your LinkedIn profile. On the top left margin look for the "Create a Group" link and submit your group. Once you have completed this task, the LinkedIn customer service department will review your submission and determine if it is an acceptable group. One thing to note here is that the submission should be done by the LinkedIn member who will be the group's administrator.

When you create a group, you have the option of adding a logo. When you upload an image, the system will automatically resize it. Unfortunately, this can sometimes lead to distortion, thereby affecting the quality and appearance of your logo. If you want to create the best logo possible, use an image editor like SnagIt, Fireworks or Photoshop.

Growing the Group

It's really easy to invite people to join your group. Simply send them an email that includes a link to your group. You can set up a list of pre-approved people who can join your group automatically upon accepting an invitation. If you want LinkedIn to automatically check the people on your "request to join" list against your pre-approved list, then make sure that the pre-approved file that you upload is 100 rows or less. Keep in mind that you need to upload these folks in .CSV format. You can add people to this list whether they are on LinkedIn or not. For those that want to be part of your group but aren't currently on LinkedIn, they will be asked to join LinkedIn. Once they become LinkedIn members, they are automatically invited to your group. If someone who is not on your pre-approved list clicks "accept," then they'll be placed in a "pending" status until you formally approve their request.

Group Size

To help manage growing groups, LinkedIn provides an ability for some extra help by enabling you to add a "Group Manager." You'll be able to quickly add or delete managers. If you want to add a manager, he or she must already be a member of the group. The person you add will also be able to manage the group from their own LinkedIn home page

Keep Your LinkedIn Group Going Even After You Leave

Sometimes things come up, priorities change, and you find yourself needing to move on. So what do you do if you need to leave? LinkedIn makes it easy for you to transfer ownership to someone else. Go to your group. Select Manage, Manage this Group, and then click on Change Owners. When you change ownership, the person you transfer it to must also be a member of the group.

36 Companies Can Play Too

One of the newest features of LinkedIn is the Company Group. In essence this is a LinkedIn profile solely for a specific Company's employees. A Company Group is a private and confidential forum where co-workers, who have been invited to join the group and who have been granted membership in the Company Group, can communicate, collaborate and stay in touch with each other. The Company Group is not open to members of LinkedIn in general; membership in a LinkedIn Company Group is by invitation only and all information is viewable only by group members. A Company Group operates akin to an intranet. On LinkedIn, the Company Group allows for a wide variety of activities such as confidential communication between group members, shared information about company business, etc.

Each formed and approved Company Group has four distinct sections:

- Members
- Updates
- News
- Q&A

Members Area – This area allows members of the Company's Group to perform searches and view profiles for other co-workers who are also members of the Company's Group.

Updates Section – In this section, members of the Company's Group can communicate with each other on virtually any topic as well as share information on the types of projects they are working on.

In "News," co-workers can see postings of Company news as well as provide comments on the news postings.

Finally, the "Q&A" section has the potential to be a pretty powerful internal communication tool. In this section, participants can post and answer questions from other co-workers, or questions that may have arisen out of company news.

One of the key issues related to a Company Group deals with eligibility. Membership in a Company Group requires a LinkedIn profile with elements from the company for which the company group has been created. These elements include:

- Your current position being with the employing company.
- Your profile must contain a valid domain name associated with the Company.
- You must have a confirmed work email address for the Company.

If you have applied for membership in the Company Group but receive an "Unconfirmed" status notice it means that a valid email address, one that is associated with your employing Company, has not been verified and/or confirmed. Once you have added a valid email address you will receive an email for confirmation. In the confirming email will be a URL link to follow in order to confirm ownership of the email address. Once this process has occurred your status will be changed to "Confirmed" for the Company Group. You can view other members of the group by clicking on the "Members" tab. Only those individuals listed under that tab will be able to view questions and answers posted in the Company Group area.

When a Company Group member leaves the employment of the sponsoring Company Group, they are no longer eligible for membership in the group. This is because membership in a Company Group is for current employees only. The former employees' status will be changed once they update their LinkedIn profile and no longer have the Company has their current employer. However, should the former employee not update their LinkedIn profile in a timely manner, the manager of the Company Group can "flag" that person's profile to indicate that they no longer work at the Company and that person's profile will be immediately removed from the company group. If the profile was flagged in error, the individual will have the opportunity to re-establish their membership by reconfirming their valid email address.

Share, Share, Share

The widgets are coming to help your professional networking and content sharing.

Back in the 1970's and 1980's when we were growing up, a widget was a generic term for a business product. However today, in our new world of social media, the term has an updated definition. Widgets are small applications that open up portals to larger applications. Across the web, you will find widgets that provide job searches, stock quotes, news, counters and much, much more. Many commercially-oriented websites such as eBay, Google, The Street.com, to name but a few, provide their own widgets.

LinkedIn also provides widgets aimed at those who want to enhance their LinkedIn experience on their blog or website. Here's what you need to do. Scroll down to the bottom of any LinkedIn page and click on the Widgets link. You'll be taken to a page where you can add the latest productivity enhancements to your site. Currently there are two Widgets available:

- Company Insider – This feature allows visitors to your site to see how they are connected to companies that you have listed on your website or blog.
- Share on LinkedIn – This widget allows visitors to share your content with their LinkedIn connections or network.

LinkedIn Widget—Company Insider

The Company Insider widget will allow users to see how they are connected to the companies that you list on your blog or website. It will show them how many people they know in total and will also supply them with a few of the names with the option of clicking on a link to see the complete list. This widget offers the best of professional networking and you can easily install it in just a few seconds.

The Company Insider Widget is offered in three different presentation formats; as a pop-up, inline with a border, or inline without a border. You can even place the widget as many times as you want on a page.

To find this widget, scroll to the bottom of any LinkedIn page and click on Widgets, then Company Insider.

LinkedIn Widget—Share on LinkedIn

Share on LinkedIn is the second free widget offered by LinkedIn. This widget allows users to share content from your website or blog with their LinkedIn network. If someone visits your website or blog where this is installed, they can literally share your content with hundreds or thousands of people they have within their own network. This can be a wonderful way to have your valuable information easily and quickly transmitted to vast audiences within someone's professional network.

This widget requires a little more coding expertise to install, but if you follow the instructions, it should be rather straightforward.

Like the Company Insider Widget, this is a wonderful tool to combine professional networking with information sharing—a true Web 2.0 application. As with the Company Insider widget, scroll to the bottom of any LinkedIn page and click on Widgets, then click on Share on LinkedIn.

38 Connect with Your Existing Tools

LinkedIn toolbars allow you to directly access LinkedIn and search from anywhere.

LinkedIn created a Toolbar that allows you to easily search the LinkedIn Network. Not only can you bookmark interesting profiles for later follow-up, but also you can save various searches. These quick and convenient toolbars work with both Internet Explorer (IE) and Firefox.

The Browser Toolbar

The LinkedIn Browser Toolbar allow you to directly access LinkedIn, search from anywhere, and also get the scoop on inside job connections. Now you can look up people instantly no matter where you are. You can search on their names, titles and other information and you can even save your searches. With one-click access to LinkedIn, you can easily see the LinkedIn profiles of everyone sending you web mail. If you're looking for a job, you'll be able to see the connections you have in your network at any hiring company where you're viewing job postings.

One feature that is part of the LinkedIn IE toolbar is the LinkedIn JobsInsider. Once you have successfully installed the LinkedIn IE toolbar, JobsInsider will be fully functional but it will be initially hidden. It will automatically show you how you are connected to job opportunities (through your own network) on various sites including Monster, CareerBuilder, Hotjobs and more.

LinkedIn also allows the user to bookmark both LinkedIn profiles as well as LinkedIn searches. This is easily achieved by clicking the "Bookmark this profile" link or choosing "Bookmark this profile" from the Bookmarks menu when viewing profiles. If for some reason you are unable to view the Bookmark Button, your toolbar might be partially hidden by Internet Explorer. If this is the case you will need to fully expand the toolbar so that the Bookmark drop-down appears.

Outlook Toolbar

The LinkedIn Outlook Toolbar offers a variety of features and functions designed to make connection with others fast and easy. What's even better is that the toolbar is absolutely free. So if you use Outlook, consider installing this time-saving, network-connecting tool.

Once you have successfully downloaded the toolbar, you can quickly upload contacts via the "Find Contacts Wizard." Please note that only those contacts in your database with a valid email address will be imported. In this procedure .CSV; .TXT and .VCF are supported file formats.

The LinkedIn Outlook Toolbar Dashboard is designed to keep in touch with your important contacts. Consider some of these benefits:

* Profile updates – You'll automatically be notified when anyone in your network updates their profile.

* Keep up-to-date – The Toolbar will also make sure that your Outlook Address Book includes the latest contact information—a great timesaver.

* Email magic – Sending a lot of emails? The Dashboard will track your activity and then make recommendations of other folks to invite to your network based on email addresses to which you're sending correspondence.

* Reminder Service – Are there contacts you haven't connected with in a while? Not to worry. The Dashboard reminder feature will let you know.

If you've installed the LinkedIn Outlook Toolbar you can easily create contact records by highlighting the contact information you want to collect and then clicking "Grab." You can add, change, or delete information after the record has been added. To save the new contact to your Outlook Address Book, click "Save and Close."

Section VII
LinkedIn—The Expanded Perspective

GOAL: Learn some interesting tidbits that may help shape your strategic perspective for using LinkedIn.

39 Separate Professional from Personal

LinkedIn is suited for maintaining an online resume of your professional credentials and for finding employers, employees, service providers, and those who can introduce you.

Social media is about communication, right? There are hundreds if not thousands of sites out on the web (and the number is growing daily) that fit the criteria for social media, but at a glance, it is very difficult to try to figure out which sites out of this jumble will be the most effective. Each of us has received those ubiquitous invitations to participate on this site or that one but the problem is, you don't know where to begin and where to focus your attention.

So it probably makes sense to categorize these sites based on function. Thus under the social media umbrella you will have categories for video/podcasting sites, photo sharing sites, social bookmarking sites and social networking sites to name just a few of the major categories. Now if we focus simply on the social networking category, there are two main sub-categories of social networks—personal and professionally-oriented. That's not to say they can't overlap but their primary missions are distinct. Using that definition, Facebook would fit under personal and LinkedIn under business.

Facebook is a different kind of tool, but just as valuable in a different way. For instance:

- Facebook shows the "whole" person—the personal side and some of the professional side, too.

- Through the use of enabling the loading of multiple pictures, Facebook facilitates additional interaction with your network.

- Facebook currently allows you to add additional content to your page.

Essentially, Facebook focuses on meeting and staying in touch with friends and sharing photos, videos and personal information. It seems suited for furthering relationships and for getting to know the "complete you." This is definitely something that can be fun but can potentially conflict with your professional ambitions if not used properly. Just think about this for a second; you post pictures on your Facebook page of that wild Happy Hour you went to with all of your friends. Sure your friends will enjoy seeing these pictures but do you really want your employer or one of your customers to see them too?

There is value to both Facebook and LinkedIn. However, LinkedIn is suited for maintaining an online resume of your professional credentials and for finding employers, employees, service providers, and those who can introduce you. In that sense, LinkedIn has an "all business" feature set and look-and-feel that are drastically different from conventional social-networking sites like Facebook, or even MySpace. While LinkedIn "is all about productivity," most of the other social networks, like Facebook, are about fun.

Not surprisingly, as many of you already know, LinkedIn has been criticized for not providing enough of a balance of promoting professional networking (also by encouraging face-to-face meetings) but as well as including information about personal life (photos, blogs, etc.).

Can Facebook be used to conduct business? The answer is, absolutely. There are definitely opportunities to create your Facebook experience to be similar to LinkedIn but make it a little more personalized. In addition, there are opportunities for leveraging their Apps framework to reach millions. Still, LinkedIn remains the more staid, business-oriented site, where people post detailed work resumes and seek recommendations about jobs.

Given these subtle differences, don't be surprised to see more, smaller, niche social networks that enable users to focus on their particular interests, careers, hobbies etc.

40 It Changes the Way We Do Things

Forty years after the Chicago Convention, social media is altering the presidential election by really giving power to the People.

We live under a form of democracy known as representative democracy, meaning our elected officials represent us. However, how such officials are elected can vary enormously. We've all heard the old cliché—every vote counts. With social media today, it gives new credence to that phrase. Never before has the common man wielded so much power with the implication of impacting the election of arguably the most powerful man in the world!

Think about this for a second. Forty years after the Chicago Convention, social media is altering the Presidential election by really giving *Power to the People.*

We are at a tipping point in our personal lives and our nation's history. Due to social media, the power of choosing the next president is undergoing an extremely unique change that is going to forever alter the way Presidential (and all political) campaigns are run.

What happened? With the convergence of technology, increased bandwidth, and the internet, literally anyone can be a one-man news feed. Whether a person is a rabble-rouser or an articulate thinker, the point is anyone can be heard and influence the masses!

Enter LinkedIn. Both John McCain and Barack Obama maintain LinkedIn profiles. In what is most likely playing to their strengths, their profiles mirror their public personas. For instance, Barack is thought of like a rock star and his popularity on LinkedIn as measured by number of connections is very high with over 20,000, making him one of the top linked people on LinkedIn. In addition, he leverages the power of communication through links to his own LinkedIn group and a link to his RSS feed.

By contrast, John McCain's profile is literally as he describes himself—a profile of straight talk. For instance, his summary is short and to the point, he has multiple recommendations from people who have worked with him and attest to his leadership. In addition, his links are to his other sites including donating to his presidential campaign.

So, what is the big takeaway here? Take a lesson from what happened during this historical presidential election. The "traditional campaign" has been completely altered and the smart candidates are the ones that have adapted to this. They are leveraging all of these new "Web 2.0" communication tools to get their message out to the masses without really having to spend much money. The ability to leverage traditional media to get the candidates message out is highly dependent on the *issue du jour*. During the 2008 Presidential election, the economic crisis dominated the headlines. Since the national nightly news on TV is only 30 minutes, this crisis severely limited the amount of coverage the candidates received which limited their ability to get their messages to the American public. In fact a lot of what was being communicated by the candidates, was being communicated by new media; web videos, blogs, and social networks. Perhaps even more importantly, the candidates were able to communicate with people that their busy campaign schedules simply wouldn't have previously permitted.

Now it's your turn to do the same thing with social media and specifically, LinkedIn. Start becoming more in-tune with what new business tools exist and how these can be integrated in your strategic business planning just as the presidential candidates are!

41 Beware of Addictive Behavior

I'm may be a LinkedIn addict, but I also have the best-connected network of anyone I know.

Disclaimer: This post is meant to be a light-hearted review of people spending too much time on LinkedIn. It is not intended to address any addictions.

If the first thing you do in the morning when you hop out of bed is to log into LinkedIn, then you may be a Link Addict (LA). If left untreated, it can lead to sleep deprivation, marital problems, and possibly generate no revenue.

10 warning signs...

If you think you are suffering from LA, take the quiz below. Just answer "true" or "false" to each statement.

1. You find yourself accessing LinkedIn, first thing in the morning, and last thing before you go to bed at night in addition to sneaking peeks during the day.

2. You become angry or agitated when your access to LinkedIn is slow or prevents you from connecting.

3. Given the choice of reading a book or spending time alone, you choose LinkedIn.

4. You check the number of "connections" you have more than once a day.

5. Your Google searches consist of finding new material related to LinkedIn.

6. You talk in terms of your friends as first, second or third level connections.

7. It makes perfect sense to you to use something called Answers to ask questions.

8. At family and/or business gatherings, you're hitting them up to see if they are on LinkedIn and interested in connecting with you.

9. You would rather spend time on LinkedIn versus spending time with your wife/family/partner/significant other (well, sometimes this might be a good thing).

10. The hair on the back of your neck stands up when someone mentions that Facebook is a social networking site for business.

If you answer "true" to one or more of these questions, you may be Linked Addicted.

Now that we have identified characteristics of a LinkedIn Addict, let's try to put a face with a name. The first person that comes to mind would be "the Doc" from the movie *Back to the Future*, all crazy-eyed and white haired, yelling to Marty about the De Lorean and the Time Continuum. On the other side of the spectrum, perhaps we may envision a young *Doogie Howser* who may have progressed from an online diary (early version of social communication) to immersing himself into the cutting edge of social media. After all as a teenage doctor, he sure had an original story to share.

It has often been said that social media addicts do not want to miss anything; they are glued to the services they use 24/7 as they feel they must have their finger on the pulse and be involved in everything and all conversations. It's almost like the old days with radio-call in contests. We all sat by the phones waiting to dial and be "the hundred and first caller." No, we couldn't dial too soon, but we had to dial quickly...and to manage this dichotomy, we needed to keep our finger on the rotary dialer (which for you young people, was what we used before voice activation).

We have populated this book with more information, more tips and more techniques for leveraging LinkedIn. So while we appreciate you reading our rules, please don't blame us if you become a Linked Addict!

42

These Are Our Rules, What Are Yours?

You've read the preceding 41 rules and now we close with our last rule. Now it is our turn to break the rules. You've read our rules, what are yours? We look forward to continuing to communicate with you. Feel free to comment on them at: http://LinkToProsper.com/24hoursuccess.

A Fast Facts—Interesting Tidbits about LinkedIn

With millions of people on LinkedIn, for those who are trivia inclined or statistical buffs, LinkedIn is rich in information. We'll take our stab at sharing some of it with you.

Fast Facts

- **Founded:** Late 2002
- **Launched:** May 1, 2003
- **Located:** Mountain View, California
- **Profitable:** Yes
- **Funded:** Yes—over $100 million
- **Investors:** Sequoia Capital (the venture investors behind Yahoo!, Google and PayPal), Bain Capital Ventures, Greylock Partners and Bessemer Ventures
- **Employees:** Over 300
- **URL:** http://linkedin.com/
- **Key Mgmt:** Dan Nye (CEO), Reid Hoffman (Founder & Chairman of the Board)
- LinkedIn's average user is 41 years old and has a household income of $109,000
- All 500 of the Fortune 500 are represented on LinkedIn
- As of November 2008, there were over 30,000,000 registered users
- Growth is 1,200,000 per month or almost 30 people per minute!

- While Facebook is bigger, LinkedIn is now growing faster. In April 2008, the number of unique visitors to LinkedIn grew by 361% over the year-earlier period, while the much larger Facebook grew by 56%, according to Nielsen Online. The largest social networking site, MySpace, by contrast, grew just 3%.

High Profile people who maintain profiles on LinkedIn include:

- Bill Gates
- John McCain
- Barack Obama
- Rudy Guiliani
- Hillary Clinton
- Ron Paul
- T. Boone Pickens
- Sir Alan Sugar (The Apprentice UK)

About 93 percent of questions asked on LinkedIn's Answers section receive answers and the first answer to a question normally is posted within an average of 9.4 hours, according to LinkedIn spokesperson Krista Canfield.

Challenges

- Although the following does not apply directly to LinkedIn, it is considered part of "Web 2.0." According to McKinsey & Company, only 21% of business executives said they are extremely or very satisfied with their company's use of Web 2.0 tools. Clearly a challenge to be addressed.

- Criticism for changes and limitations placed on its users including not showing the actual number of connections (i.e. LinkedIn only shows 500+ as opposed to the actual number), restricting membership to no more than 50 groups and limiting the total number or invitations.

B The Crystal Ball – What Might LinkedIn do in the Future?

This is probably the $1 billion question that LinkedIn is answering internally and boy do we wish we had a crystal ball to forecast this! Let's start our analysis for this by looking at a possible strategic direction the company may entertain and progress with our analysis down to the user level.

Clearly, by raising capital, LinkedIn is looking to grow and its investors are looking for a high priced exit that rewards them for their investment. With that being said, there have been rumors that Microsoft is a natural fit to provide an exit solution.

Three interesting points to ponder:

- In the future Microsoft wants to bump up against Google in paid search, and it needs to reach the right demographics. Enter LinkedIn with its millions of—mostly white-collar—professionals.

- Microsoft is planning to battle Google in cloud computing to keep its Office applications suite relevant and, once again, it wouldn't hurt to have millions of professionals (and adults) on its side.

- And perhaps more important is for a defensive play. If LinkedIn fits so well under Microsoft, how great would it look under the Google umbrella?

Business Development

Research & Development – LinkedIn is in the process of opening its site to outside software developers, something Facebook did to great fanfare. Through our research, we understand that LinkedIn has been focusing on a developer platform. This holds great potential if developed out in line with LinkedIn's white-collar crowd.

Premium Memberships – Think about the "velvet rope." Back in the 1970's, at Studio 54, everyone wanted to be on the inside of that rope. The desire to get on the inside of that rope and achieve "status" transformed Studio 54 into "the place to be go and be seen." LinkedIn can do something similar. If traditional networking can be considered stale, LinkedIn has an amazing opportunity to target those users who want status and want to connect with the business elite. LinkedIn can transform their Premium memberships from the bland to status symbols and cater to the business elite as well as the power user just like American Express has done with the Amex Black card.

Business Partnerships – Back in March 2008, LinkedIn announced a partnership with Businessweek.com and Capital IQ to tie in their proprietary data with LinkedIn's Company Profiles. This is just one of many data tie-ins that could greatly benefit business partners. Shifting our perspective on business verticals, what if LinkedIn partnered with some of the ERP vendors and provided any number of simple enterprise software features? While we are not infrastructure experts, we could sure let our mind wander. It would be an interesting and fun exercise to imagine all the types of solutions that LinkedIn could provide here. Interestingly, LinkedIn can harvest their own data to facilitate the development of their business partnerships as top business people from all of the Fortune 500, along with other potentially relevant business partners, are already members of LinkedIn.

We look forward to watch the development of LinkedIn and see if it delivers on the promise it currently has to alter business communications.

C 42 Things You Can Do with LinkedIn

Early in the book, we asked you how you were looking to utilize LinkedIn. To help you answer that, we have provided a variety of perspectives from Executives to Small Businesses to Job Seekers to functional things you can do. So without further ado, here are 42 things you can do with LinkedIn.

1. Answer the question of why you are on LinkedIn
2. Update and expand your profile
3. (Better yet) Do an extreme makeover on your profile!
4. Create your "3-second elevator pitch"
5. Customize your URL
6. Leverage the power of SEO by filling in your specialties with effective phrases
7. Write recommendations
8. Ask for recommendations
9. Find an expert
10. Ask and answer questions
11. Ask for an introduction from one of your direct connections to someone they are directly connected to
12. Educate people on how and why you want to be contacted
13. Become adept at using the Search Function
14. Join and participate in a couple of relevant groups

15. Organize a group based around an area of interest to you
16. Continue to grow your connections and build a quality network
17. Set up the Outlook Toolbar
18. Leverage the LinkedIn Widgets

Functional Uses:

19. Market your company
20. Use LinkedIn for Market Research
21. Gather business intelligence on your competitors
22. Career Management
23. Job Search
24. Recruiting
25. Keeping in Touch
26. Find Business Partners, Vendors and Clients
27. Revise existing business processes
28. Establishing an introduction that leads to Meeting Face-to-Face

Three ways for IT professionals to use LinkedIn with their Internal Customers:

29. Connect with and build relationships within your company
30. Communicate what you are working to your users
31. Generate recommendations from your users – builds internal credibility

Three ways Executives can use LinkedIn:
32. Job search (just like everyone else)
33. Research and land board positions
34. Conversely, they can attract key employees, partners and suppliers

Three ways Small Businesses can leverage the power of communication:
35. Use the LinkedIn database to understand more about your prospects and how people you currently know can assist in connecting you
36. Notify your contacts of significant news, prospects, closings, sales, opportunities, etc.

37. Stay current on what your business partners, vendors, former colleagues and potential new recruits are up to in their professional lives

Three ways for Job Seekers to leverage LinkedIn:

38. Check out LinkedIn jobs

39. Use LinkedIn to find relevant headhunters to talk to

40. Use LinkedIn to expand the network of people you already know and keep them abreast of your search

And in closing...

41. Play by the rules—don't abuse, don't invent, don't circumvent

42. Lastly, regardless of the preceding 41 things, make time for your wife or significant other. We won't go into what can happen if you don't

For more information and tips, please remember that you can always go to http://LinkToProsper.com/24hoursuccess

D 42 Rules In Action—Products & Services to Help You

Some of us who read this book may not have the time to build their LinkedIn experience to where they want it to be, while others simply want just a bit of additional guidance. We offer a variety of options to help your success at: http://LinkToProsper.com

This includes our free companion workbook to these 42 Rules at: http://LinkToProsper.com/24hoursuccess

Other products and services are available for purchase at http://LinkToProsper.com/Products. This includes:

- *For those who are looking to build success habits but don't have much time to spend*

  - 21 Day Program to LinkedIn Success – Only 15 minutes per day

- *Your profile is your fundamental cornerstone for your LinkedIn experience. For those who want someone to completely redo their profile, we offer:*

  - The "Extreme Makeover"

  Others have a strong profile but simply want some tips on where it can be fine tuned, and for that we offer:

  - A 30 Point Profile Assessment

- *There are a variety of user types on LinkedIn and whereas some people like to learn through books, others are more comfortable with video instruction. Therefore we offer the following downloadable Webinars:*

  - **LinkedIn-troduction** – Good starting point for new users
  - **Get Started Now** – For those who have been on LinkedIn for a while but desire a clearer focus on what they wish to achieve now

- *People like to keep their knowledge sharp and participating in a virtual group coaching, ala a mini-mastermind, offers flexibility, interactivity and of course, idea generation. Some promote Group Think, but our 6–8 person groups are called "Group Link"*

  - **Group Link**

About the Authors

Chris Muccio is an award-winning entrepreneur who draws upon insightful experiences from his successful career in Corporate America to guide business leaders on the most effective strategies to uncover profit and growth opportunities resulting in rapid and sustainable improvements within their business. His insight on social networking is highly sought after.

David Burns has been the founder of three companies, two of which were in the telecommunications industry. In these endeavors, he was instrumental in raising over $15 million in private equity as well as raising senior debt and working capital revolvers. David started his career with Ernst and Young, LLP where he worked on audits of both public and private companies.

Peggy Murrah is the owner of a highly successful web design and virtual assistance business, providing her clients with resources to succeed in the online world of business. Through her ongoing networking, she created strong business relationships with entrepreneurs across diverse industries, and facilitated many mutually beneficial connections among them.

Write Your Own Rules

You can write your own 42 Rules book, and we can help you do it—from initial concept, to writing and editing, to publishing and marketing. If you have a great idea for a 42 Rules book, then we want to hear from you.

As you know, the books in the 42 Rules series are practical guidebooks that focus on a single topic. The books are written in an easy-to-read format that condenses the fundamental elements of the topic into 42 Rules. They use realistic examples to make their point and are fun to read.

Two Kinds of 42 Rules Books

42 Rules books are published in two formats: the single-author book and the contributed-author book. The single-author book is a traditional book written by one author. The contributed-author book (like *42 Rules for Working Moms*) is a compilation of Rules, each written by a different contributor, which support the main topic. If you want to be the sole author of a book or one of its contributors, we can help you succeed!

42 Rules Program

A lot of people would like to write a book, but only a few actually do. Finding a publisher, and distributing and marketing the book are challenges that prevent even the most ambitious of authors to ever get started.

At 42 Rules, we help you focus on and be successful in the writing of your book. Our program concentrates on the following tasks so you don't have to:

- **Publishing:** You receive expert advice and guidance from the Executive Editor, copy editors, technical editors, and cover and layout designers to help you create your book.

- **Distribution:** We distribute your book through the major book distribution channels, like Baker & Taylor and Ingram, Amazon.com, Barnes and Noble, Borders Books, etc.

- **Marketing:** 42 Rules has a full-service marketing program that includes a customized Web page for you and your book, email registrations and campaigns, blogs, webcasts, media kits and more.

Whether you are writing a single-authored book or a contributed-author book, you will receive editorial support from 42 Rules Executive Editor, Laura Lowell, author of *42 Rules of Marketing*, which was rated Top 5 in Business Humor and Top 25 in Business Marketing on Amazon.com (December 2007), and author and Executive Editor of *42 Rules for Working Moms*.

Accepting Submissions

If you want to be a successful author, we'll provide you the tools to help make it happen. Start today by answering the following questions and visit our website at http://superstarpress.com/ for more information on submitting your 42 Rules book idea.

Super Star Press is now accepting submissions for books in the 42 Rules book series. For more information, email: info@superstarpress.com or call 408-257-3000.

A Message From Super Star Press™

Thank you for your purchase of this 42 Rules Series book. It is available online at: http://42rules.com/24_hour_success_with_linkedin/ or at other online and physical bookstores. To learn more about contributing to books in the 42 Rules series, check out http://superstarpress.com.

Please contact us for quantity discounts at sales@superstarpress.com

If you want to be informed by email of upcoming books, please email bookupdate@superstarpress.com.

Printed in the United States
138993LV00009B/29/P